BENDING THE CURVE

BENDING THE CURVE:

Applying Lean Systems Thinking to Government and Service Organizations

WALTER LOWELL & ARTHUR DAVIS

Palmetto Publishing Group
Charleston, SC

Bending the Curve
Copyright © 2020 by Walter Lowell and Arthur Davis
All rights reserved

No portion of this book may be reproduced, stored in a retrieval system, or transmitted in any form by any means–electronic, mechanical, photocopy, recording, or other except for brief quotations in printed reviews, without prior permission of the author.

First Edition

Printed in the United States

Paperback: 978-1-64990-173-6
eBook: 978-1-64990-172-9

This is dedicated to Richard Lowell, a promise fulfilled, and to my lovely wife Linda, and children Christine, Jim and Alyson with love for their patience and support.

Arthur S. Davis Senior, your heart of gold, native wisdom and love is still missed! Thanks for your faith in me!

TABLE OF CONTENTS

FOREWORD

One of the great ironies of government is that while it guards its citizenry against the threats posed by monopolies, it is itself a monopoly. Competition and choice for buyers of goods and services drive prices down, cost out, and innovation up. In this way, for-profit corporations actually benefit from the presence of viable alternatives to their own products and services because they must constantly improve or fall behind.

Government, as a public service monopoly, typically does not have the opportunity to enjoy the same benefits from the presence of competitive alternatives. If I need a driver's license, a building permit, or assistance from the Department of Environmental Protection, there is only one place to go. The speed, quality, and cost of those experiences are determined by government alone. Consumer choice is most often absent from the government services marketplace.

As importantly, and as a result, the employees of government can often have a work experience that is rigid, bureaucratic, and slow to change. Picture an image of a government office building. Are the lights a little dimmer? Are the computers a little heavier? Are the steel or wooden desks a little thicker and older? While certainly there are many exceptions, this is a template that frequently comes to mind. Public sector work plays out in an environment of less competition and buyer choice, and while lots of high-value activity is delivered each day, as a whole the world of work in government is ripe for great change.

Fortunately, there is a road map to an alternate reality, and this book lays it out. Government institutions have the same potential for innovation and quality as all other organizations. Human beings, wherever they are present, are capable of creating exceptional results! But there must be a framework for guiding that activity toward a fresh vision in which spending less time and money actually creates more social value. The government model of work is framed by the government model of budgeting. Often there is pressure within that system to spend all the money allotted to ensure an equal or expanding allotment the following fiscal year. But beyond the world of government, it is well understood, that more spending does not directly correlate to higher quality. Often, the two are inversely related. As organizations become lean, the resources required are reduced and capital is freed to flow to other areas of new need and opportunity.

In their book, *BENDING THE CURVE: Applying Lean Systems Thinking to Government and Service Organizations*, Walter Lowell and Arthur Davis offer a fresh path to dynamic government filled with exciting jobs that are surrounded by innovation, waste elimination, process improvement, and happy customers. Lean systems thinking is a tried, tested, and proven template for organizational excellence. This is achieved by creating a culture that empowers everyone in the organization to find and eliminate waste while focusing on delivering just the value the customer is willing to pay for. When this magic occurs, organizations thrive, and the jobs within them become exceptionally dynamic and rewarding!

My name is Kevin Hancock, and I am the CEO of Hancock Lumber Company, one of the oldest businesses in America. Our company was established in 1848, and today we have 550 employee team members working across Maine. In 2001 we began our own "Lean journey" with an initial workshop at our sawmill in Bethel. Back then we were certain we were already lean and that the training wasn't really necessary. Our company had been successful for generations, and surely, we knew more about our unique industry than our facilitators did. "This is the lumber business," we thought to ourselves. "Our industry is different." Little did we know how much change could be created by learning to give every employee a voice and a tool kit for identifying and eliminating waste and focusing on the customer.

My personal learning in leading a lean organization was accelerated in 2010 when I acquired a rare neurological voice disorder called spasmodic dysphonia that made speaking difficult. As CEO, my voice was my primary tool, and suddenly I couldn't really use it. During that time people at work would come to me with a question or a problem, and because I knew I was not going to be able to speak well enough to give a detailed answer, I started responding by simply saying, "That's a great question. What do you think we should do about it?" The person I was talking to would then give his or her opinion, and I would typically follow by saying, "That sounds good; let's go do that." And off they would go with his or her solution to the identified problem.

After months and then years of these exchanges, it struck me that people at work typically didn't need a CEO-centric (or supervisory-centric) answer to most of their questions. People already knew what to do. They just needed the encouragement and support to trust their judgment and act. It was in this way that I became obsessed with a fresh leadership strategy that pushed power out and away from the center and gave every member of the team a voice. This is the essence of Lean systems thinking.

As of today, Hancock Lumber has been designated as one of the "Best Places to Work in Maine" for six years in a row. We are one of just a few manufacturers and a handful of retailers to make the list. The secret to that accomplishment lies in the creation of a leadership culture that disperses power instead of collects it. Lean systems thinking, training, and tools are essential ingredients in the journey to empower everyone within an organization.

Government entities have equal access to these tools and an equal opportunity to create an exceptional work environment driven by highly engaged employees who are driving out waste and using their voice to create change. Walter Lowell and Arthur Davis see this potential and have invested years of work introducing Lean strategies to Maine state government. Their book is a gift that has recorded their triumphs, failures, experiences, and strategies for bringing Lean thinking into the halls of government for the betterment of all citizens, especially those working within government.

Government in some form exists everywhere there is a community on this planet. Its power and potential for good are virtually limitless, but achieving that performance zenith requires change. That change needs a framework, and this book provides it. Enjoy!

Kevin Hancock
September 2019

The aim should be to work on the method of management.
—W. Edwards Deming

PREFACE

In 2004 and unknown to each other, the authors had begun to actively explore the use of Lean systems thinking in their respective departments of Maine state government: Maine Departments of Labor (MDOL) and Health and Human Services (DHHS). We eventually joined forces later that year, and the interdepartmental *Bend the Curve* (*BTC*) was born. *BTC* was initiated at the time to offer a unique alternative to managing budgets by simultaneously focusing on lowering the cost and improving government services. Moreover, through *BTC* the authors set their sights on changing the culture of government work by specifically adapting and deploying Lean principles and methods that were proven to work so successfully in manufacturing.

> The term "Lean/continuous improvement" is defined as incremental improvement of products, processes, and services over time, with the goal of reducing waste to improve workplace functionality, customer service, and/or product performance. Lean is founded on the concepts of continuous and incremental improvements on product and process while eliminating redundant activities and increasing respect for people.

This is the story of that journey in which *BTC* created a unique system that offered a new way to engage staff and manage and improve government operations designed to be better, faster, and cheaper. The authors are indebted to many people for making this happen. This book is not an exposition on Lean principles and methods, for there are many of those already in print (see the appended references section). Rather, it explores the challenges of designing, developing, customizing, and deploying a Lean management system designed for manufacturing into a government/service environment. Governments play a critical role in our lives, and it is important that we continually seek ways to improve them. We discuss the success and failures of this endeavor, and lessons learned, and hope that interested readers will benefit from what we have learned and leaders of government operations and their citizens everywhere will benefit from this work.

At the August 2016 annual Lean Systems Summit in Portland, Maine, the keynote speaker, Jim Womack, lamented that his one regret in his Lean journey was giving the name "Lean" to the Toyota Production System (TPS) that he and his team, including Daniel T. Jones and Daniel Roos, were studying. He noted that of all the manufacturing systems they reported on in their book *The Machine that Changed the World*, Toyota was using less of everything: less time, less money, less space, less people. Pondering a way to describe this system his research team agreed that it was "leaner" than all the other systems they had studied. The name stuck, and thus the term "Lean" became the name to describe Toyota's remarkable business system.

Regrettably, the name "Lean" has taken on considerable baggage since then. Often, rather than signaling a remarkable and innovative way to run an organization, it is often seen as something threatening—primarily because in its early adoption in the United States of America, "Lean" was frequently used as a means or set of tools to lay people off. Unfortunately, one of the most powerful systems invented to effectively manage an organization often remains largely misunderstood, carrying misconceptions, or remains in the margins of understanding of organizations that could benefit from it. While manufacturing companies worldwide have come to see the value of Lean, it is only slowly being discovered in the world outside of manufacturing—in part, because there is so much misunderstanding associated with the term "Lean." One of the first and often biggest barriers to any organization in achieving excellence is getting beyond the term "Lean" that Womack and his coauthors so innocently coined many years ago.

In his keynote, Womack went on to emphasize that Lean was a "business system," not just a set of tools. It can be applied to any organization, public or private, that is seeking to improve its culture and operations. Fundamentally, it is teaching employees to identify problems and use experiments to find solutions to these problems, however big or small they may be. This is the foundation of A-3 thinking and the Plan Do Study Act (PDSA) cycle Lean practitioners are so familiar with (i.e., the relentless application of science to the problems of the workplace). Womack went on to note that Lean is managing by science—not to be confused with, for example, the scientific management of Taylorism. At the end of the summit, he talked about Lean as experimenting and as a way of learning something new—that even a failed experiment can help us learn something we had not known before. Equally important is documenting this learning so that others may benefit, thus enabling an organization to learn and improve.

Jim Womack's words came as an auspicious inspiration for the authors because the annual Lean Systems Summit was conceived as part of the State of Maine's Bend the Curve program. *BTC* was designed to apply Lean principles and methods to government operations. Unfortunately, four years earlier, as the Summit Planning Team was putting the finishes touches on the summit program and after eight years of *BTC* operation, orders came to us that *BTC* was to cease and desist all work and that even the term "Lean" was *not* to be used again in the current state government administration. While not entirely unexpected from this administration, it was baffling and a shock to the *BTC* team. How could a business system that is designed to improve operations, and had demonstrated it did so in Maine state government, be so thoroughly rejected? Even more surprising was that in 2011 Harvard University's Ash Center for Democratic Governance and Innovation at the John F. Kennedy School of Government announced its recognition of the Innovative State of Maine Bend the Curve program as a Bright Idea award recipient, stating: "Maine's Bend the Curve program has demonstrated that Lean methods and principles work in government, are enthusiastically embraced by employees and offer a unique and innovative opportunity to transform government" (see appendix F).

This past decision was a fitting punctuation point to Jim Womack's closing words on experimentation at the Lean Summit and also a starting point for the authors to document the Bend the Curve experiment in Maine state government, so others might benefit from what we learned, both successes and failures. This book describes the *BTC* story

> **Chapter one** describes the rationale for developing *BTC* and using Lean in state government. We discuss why it is important for state government (government in general) to alter its current culture of "blame/shame" to one that is focused on systems and processes.
> **Chapter two** describes how Bend the Curve got started and the challenges and events that enabled it to get off the ground. It also discusses adapting a Lean manufacturing model to government services and our launch strategy.

Chapter three discusses how and why we created and trained continuous improvement practitioners (CIPs). CIPs played a key role in Bend the Curve and proved to be very successful in understanding and facilitating improvements.

Chapter four describes the program design and model we used to develop CIPs, how we recruited them, and the abilities they needed to be successful.

Chapter five discusses the standard materials we developed to enable CIPs to be successful in the field.

Chapter six discusses the issue of sustaining *BTC* and the various strategies we developed to sustain Lean thinking in government and, in effect, to change the culture of government. *BTC* sought to instill knowledge and expertise in state government so that we would no longer need to rely on expensive external consultants but rather build expert Lean capacity into the government culture that would remain as administrations changed.

Chapter seven describes the results *BTC* achieved from these efforts. These include both qualitative changes as well as quantitative improvements.

Chapter eight provides a summary of *BTC* and describes the lessons learned.

The **epilogue** is a final statement about *BTC* and its legacy.

Management's job is to improve the system.
—W. Edwards Deming

CHAPTER 1: INTRODUCTION

Maine is a small state sitting in the northeast corner of New England. It borders Canada to the north, the Atlantic Ocean to the east, and New Hampshire to the south and west. Maine has a small, aging population of approximately 1.3 million people, mostly living in its urban centers and southern counties. Historically, its economy was based on forestry and fishing, with a small manufacturing sector; all contribute significantly to the state's tax base and budget. Maine is called "Vacationland" because of its vast forests, many lakes and rivers, and its extensive and beautiful coastline. As a result, a significant percentage of its economy is also based on tourism. Over the last three decades, Maine's economy has suffered considerably with significant losses due to globalization in the paper industry, high tech, and reductions in fishing due to overfishing and a warming ocean. As of this writing, the shutdown imposed by the Corona virus has further devastated Maine's economy. As a result, state government has and is currently seeing a loss of revenue that requires hard choices by government administrators to reduce taxes, budgets, and programs while demand for services has remain unabated or increased. Several strategies have been deployed to meet these challenges, including reductions in the state workforce, pay freezes, and furloughs—all done to help manage the loss of revenue.

There have also been efforts to manage the state's budget by attempting innovative strategies used in the business sector and applied to government operations. Over the last three decades, spanning four different government administrations, there has been some form of improvement methodology deployed in government operations. In the early 80s, a time when the economy in Maine was suffering considerably, the McKernan administration, in order to balance the state budget, began by furloughing the state workforce as well as ordering across-the-board budget reductions. In addition, a statewide total quality management (TQM) program for government was instituted. The central focus of the program was to reduce costs by removing waste in government services. TQM was an "all hands-on deck" initiative involving the hiring of TQM consultants, a W. Edwards Deming four-day workshop for managers, and the training of staff on TQM principles and methods. TQM was implemented across all state departments with each department designating a TQM lead and creating a TQM plan of action, with responsibility for the plan resting with the department director or commissioner. The governor chaired a statewide quality council, consisting of the line staff designated as TQM leads and their respective directors or commissioners, which met regularly to check on progress. This was a very exciting time for state employees.

They received a lot of TQM training, were engaged with their work, were listened to by management, and had opportunities to work across different departments on quality improvement projects. It was encouraging to the workforce to see the governor take an active and visible role in promoting their participation and seeking to improve state operations. This effort occurred in the last two years of the McKernan administration, and unfortunately, there was not enough time to build or embed a solid internal administrative infrastructure to support TQM. The TQM consultant was only on board for a little more than a year, and the Lean and Continuous Improvement literature at that time was not robust enough to fully articulate for government some of the very important improvement tools/methodologies such as visual management, value stream mapping, and *hoshin* planning—to name a few—that would help to sustain an ongoing improvement effort.

Typical Government Improvement Strategies

Ken Miller, in *We Don't Make Widgets: Overcoming the Myths that Keep Government from Radically Improving*, notes some of the strategies government typically deploys to improve its operations:

- The Blue Ribbon Commission
- Centralization/decentralization
- Reorganization
- Blame the Individual (i.e., performance management)
- More technology

These are strategies we have become familiar with over our years in state service. We agree with Miller's assessment that generally "they never actually work."

Recent Maine State Government Administrations

John McKernan (R) 1987–1995
Angus King (I) 1995–2003
John Baldacci (D) 2003–2012
Paul LePage (R) 2012–2019
Janet Mills (D) 2019–

In Maine, the governor is elected every four years and is termed out in eight. When the next administration takes over, not surprisingly it often comes with policy initiatives of its own and looks to make its own mark on state operations that is generally different from the previous administration's. While the TQM program was still in operation with the election of the King administration, the economy had stabilized somewhat, and unfortunately, TQM was not seen as a priority by the new administration. The governor decided to relegate the overall responsibility for TQM away from the governor's office to a Labor Relations Committee, which, in effect, killed TQM as an overall government-supported initiative. Surprisingly, this was a governor who ran on the idea of managing government as a business, and yet, when he was presented with a successful world class business strategy its potential went unrecognized.

Although some departments continued with improvement efforts such as zero-based budgeting, the lack of executive support, particularly for TQM, was obvious to the state workforce. It seemed to many involved in the TQM effort as a betrayal, as well as an immense loss of momentum coupled with a growing cynicism and suspicion of any new government program "foisted" on the state workforce. Unfortunately, this persisted into the administration that followed as did a return of serious challenges to the economy.

A confluence of issues occurred at the start of the next administration. These included a return of significant budget deficits and unhappy citizens demanding a smaller government and more accountability. It was in this environment that the *BTC* initiative emerged in 2004, largely because of a few state employees who continued to follow the quality improvement literature, particularly those strategies called *Lean*, which were being successfully deployed in manufacturing companies around the world and were clearly articulated in the Womack and Jones book, *Lean Thinking*, published in 2003. Given another strained economy and considerable stress on the state budget, the new administration again resorted to the same timeworn playbook of across-the-board budget reductions, staff layoffs, and reorganizing/consolidating state departments—all designed to reduce costs.

Government services, programs, and projects greatly affect the competitive position, progress, and future of the entire society.[1] The decision to continue to

1 Frank T. Anbari, *Aligning Six Sigma Strategy with Current Department Initiatives*. George Washington University.

ignore the problem of waste in the government service system is a decision that affects Maine's standing not only in the state of Maine but also in the world. Even the leadership position of the United States is also adversely affected by dramatic ineffectiveness and inefficiencies at the state level.

Declining resources is not the only challenge confronting state governments; of equal consequence is the productivity of their service components. Studies have found that, from the customer's perspective, there is 30 to 80 percent waste in government systems.[2] *BTC*, the innovative program developed in Maine state government, recognized the importance of public value specific to public institutions. A public service organization generates public value when it delivers a set of social and economic outcomes that are aligned with citizens' priorities in a cost-effective manner. Thus, maximizing outcomes and organizational cost-effectiveness increases the value it delivers.[3]

BTC demonstrated that government workers can meet the challenge of declining resources and can do more with less while both delighting their customers and increasing public value to society. However, to embed a continuous improvement culture, governmental leaders and workers must study and use the twenty-first-century leadership/management systems now in use by successful manufacturing companies, hospitals, accounting firms, engineering firms, and others in the service sector.

A Different Kind of Thinking

Government does not need to invent a system. The Toyota Production System (TPS) already exists, but the adoption of this system of leadership and management requires a fundamental change in our current thinking and methods, and it requires a different kind of leadership. Leaders who believe that if manufacturers can dramatically reduce costs, radically improve customer satisfaction, and quadruple the level of quality while providing the investor (i.e. taxpayers) with an enhanced performance, so can government and other service sector entities. The inefficiency, cost, and dissatisfaction that citizens have with current government operations represent "a burning platform," a reason for change that cannot be ignored.

There are clear and strong parallels between government and the private sector:

---

2 Michael L. George, *Lean Six Sigma for Service*. McGraw-Hill, 2003.

3 Martin Cole and Greg Parson, *Unlocking Public Value*. Accenture, all rights reserved (source internet, 10–29–07).

Parallels between Government and Private Business*		
Accountability	Business	Government
	Investors	**Taxpayers**
	Board of Directors	**Legislature or Government Board**
	CEO	**Governor or County Commissioner/ Town Mayor**
	Business Unit	**Department or Division**
	Products/Services	**Products/Services**

* Adapted from Ken Miller. *We Don't Make Widgets: Overcoming the Myths That Keep Government from Radically Improving*. Washington, DC: Governing Books, 2006.

Transformational Change

Change of this magnitude requires a deep commitment to fundamentally transform every element of government operations—how and what employees and managers think about them, what the system does, and how it rewards, measures, and executes its processes. This is transformational change, not simply a project implementation. The solution is far-reaching, dramatic, and challenging, but it is needed and, more importantly, very doable—as *BTC* demonstrated by saving $35,077,079 (see details in appendix A) in bona fide savings and improved quality, delivery time, and customer and employee satisfaction in the participating Maine state government agencies, which comprised 65 percent of the Maine state government's workforce.

However, there was and continues to be a critical shortage of public administration leaders and managers who (1) believe that operations are what they were hired to pay attention to and (2) seek the necessary learning to make the transformation and 3) have a sound understanding of system/process thinking. We believe that this is the case because many have no understanding of what operations really demands of them, are discouraged from trying new things, and/or often have low morale due to constant leadership changes and downsizing threats, real and imagined.

We must stop defining the government system of work as a series of discrete events and tasks and accept Deming's statement that "all work is a process," defined as a combination of people, resources, and methods that produce a result. It is a method that transforms inputs into outputs to satisfy customers (the direct recipient) with the aim of creating value added outcomes. In business, one outcome is profits. In government it is public value, a reflection of the collective benefit for the recipients of government products and services. Unfortunately, many if not most government employees, line staff and managers, do not think of work in terms of process and continuous improvement.

The work in government and the service sector reveals no real distinction between the work of government and a manufacturing company. Ken Miller in his book *We Don't Make Widgets* exploded the myth that government is somehow different than private enterprise. Miller emphasized that both have customers, products, processes, and outputs—although both use different terms to describe them. Until government managers and workers realize this similarity, they are blind to the valuable lessons learned in manufacturing and the private sector that have led to astounding improvements in how products and services are delivered.

TPS and Lean

The Toyota Production System (TPS) often referred to as "Lean" has become the leadership and management system of choice in the twenty-first century. In the Toyota system all activities relating to the process of doing business, whatever that business might be, are either classified as "adding value" or "creating waste." Limiting or managing two or more of these activities, for example managing wastes—in time, in excess inventory, and space—reduces cost. However, all too often today public service managers fall into the same trap that many manufacturers fell into twenty to thirty years ago. They narrow their focus on fixing parts of the system, rather than implementing fundamental change to the system itself. Only a robust transformation of the whole system will result in the dramatic change needed and, as importantly, ensure sustainability. This is what Lean thinking is all about.

All Work Is a Process

BTC sought to apply TPS/Lean to state government. Lean was initially believed to be a manufacturing leadership and management method. However, this limited appreciation for the universality of Lean is recognized as misleading. Lean is applicable in any business sector. The underpinning of Lean is Deming's "all work is a process." Given that this is the case, then, "we all have customers, processes can be defined, methods can be standardized, and processes can be measured."[4]

---

4 Dr. Joseph Juran. National Technical University (NTU) "Quest for Quality" and NTU Special Series "Quality Improvement as a Business Strategy." @1989 William E. Eureka. Tuesday, October 24, 1989. Pages 5 of 137 and 54 of 137 of the October 1989 slide presentation.

Government, and any other transactional or service-centered entity, has multiple functions; for government the one that is most readily accepted and most recognizable is the function that creates laws, policies, and rules. The other function is its operational elements that convert those laws, policies, and rules into action that can be put into practice.

The primary function of operational elements is to transform the legislative and governmental initiatives and programs into services, products, and actions. These are what constitute the output of the process. Figure 1.1 displays this relationship.

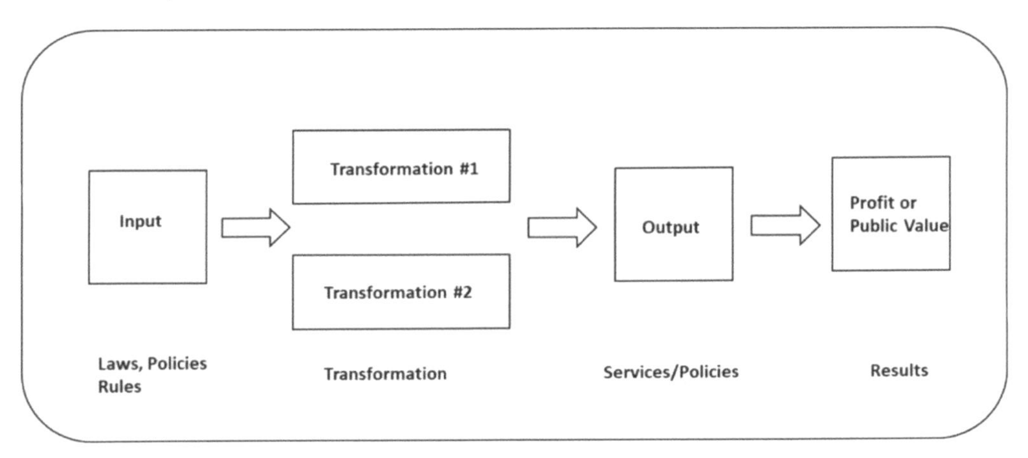

Figure 1.1

Making the Connections

The pursuit of *BTC* was not merely a cost-cutting exercise focused on making government smaller or creating fewer jobs but an exercise focused on creating a government enterprise that routinely meets the lofty expectations of continuously doing more, doing it better, and doing it for less.

BTC sought to improve government performance with the least amount of resources while producing profound and continuously improved products and services delivered to the customer. Moreover, these outcomes were not achieved at the expense of the worker; indeed, the worker took on a critical role of being the key resource for change. Of equal importance, *BTC* sought to produce an environment where continuous and deliberate improvement was the norm. When achieved, operational excellence becomes the norm—that is, the organization would continuously increase effectiveness and efficiency and thus improve productivity and quality of service. Productivity means, even in the public sector, output per resource applied.

When we began to undertake the changes necessary to implement *BTC*, we were embarking on a journey. As we implemented the initial phase of the journey, we sought to establish a robust operating system that is led by leaders dedicated to achieving nothing less than true operational excellence.

Government has often been asked to do more with less, but today the stakes are higher than ever. "American government faces a productivity imperative. Growth in program size, new national priorities, and citizens' demand for increased choice, convenience, and customer service will require government to do more and do it better—and all of this in an era of, at best, constant levels of spending."[5]

In the June 2006 issue of the *McKinsey Quarterly Review*, authors Nina Bhatia and John Drew defined an operating system as the configuration of assets, material resources, and staff needed to *produce output for a direct recipient*, the customer. In so doing, its outcome is focused on adding value and eliminating waste as defined by the customer. The system of Operational Excellence, or Lean production, as it is more popularly known, is a combination of tools, evaluation, internal connection with Lean thinking at the core.[6]

A robust operating system is likely to be comprised of 80 percent operations (the management of assets, material resources, and staff) and 20 percent the creation component of the system. The creation component consists of visioning methods, strategy development, policy creation, et cetera. Today, the operating system of government appears, instead, to be 80 percent policy creation, program and/or grant management, and relations building; 20 percent budget and staffing management; and 0 percent formal operations management. Given that the 80/20 percent balance of a robust operating system is not in place, the fundamental work for the needed change begins with the establishment and development of a new mindset. A key design principle behind *BTC* was to establish a "process mindset" in government managers and workers.

The Hidden Tax.

Yet, the question remains: Why adopt a new system? Why would government leaders, managers, or workers want to increase productivity? The answer is threefold:

- The first concern is the here and now. Government's current environment demands it.

---

5 Tony Danker, Thomas Dohrmann, Nancy Killefer, and Lenny Mendonca, "How Can American Government Meet Its Productivity Challenges?" *McKinsey Quarterly Review* (2006).

6 Jamie Flinchbaugh and Andy Carlino quoted in *The Hitchhiker's Guide to Lean: Lessons from the Road* (Dearborn, Michigan: Society of Manufacturing Engineers, 2006).

- Second, there is always more demand than resources to meet it, thus requiring increased productivity.
- Third, the resources that government use cannot be treated as if they are infinite, rather than finite.
- Fourth, waste is a 'hidden tax' applied to the cost of all government services.

Here in Maine, as no doubt elsewhere, the current reality finds that most citizens believe that they are overtaxed, government is doing a poor job providing products and services, waste is endemic, and government is unable to provide exactly what its customers, the citizens, are looking for when in need.

Others have shown that the cost in the service sector (government, marketing, sales, accounting, hospitals, banking, et cetera) are inflated by 30 to 80 percent; that is, the processes are riddled with activities that add no value from the perspective of the customer. As Henry Ford noted years ago, "Many people are busy trying to find better ways of doing things that should not have to be done at all. There is no progress in merely finding a better way to do a useless thing."[7]

Government needs to do better. Public expectations are increasing, for better schools and better health care, less crime, and more efficient systems. In addition, there is a need to provide new services to support changing household structures and build new skills in the workplace in the face of globalization. As a result, governments need to improve their effectiveness significantly, which means finding evermore innovative ways of delivering better public service.[8]

Unfortunately, in Maine it is a highly likely that mounting challenges are yet to come. For instance, Maine's aging population "will require government to expand already overburdened health-care and retirement programs."[9] These concerns can be resolved, in part, by radically improving the efficiency and effectiveness (productivity) of government.

Operational Excellence

Is change of this magnitude possible? The answer is a resounding, "Yes." Where does our confidence come from? It comes from the knowledge that others, leaders, managers, and laypeople, working in the private sector have changed their way of work and from the work we describe here in this book. Does the work of the

7 Michael L. George, *Lean Six Sigma for Service: How to Use Lean Speed and Six Sigma Quality to Improve Service and Transitions* (The McGraw-Hill Cos., 2003).

8 Michael Babar, Alastair Levy, and Lenny Mendonca, "Global Trends Affecting the Public Sector," *McKinsey Quarterly Review* (2007).

9 Ibid., 6.

private sector parallel that of government? Do the same rules and methods apply? Those are the same questions that some manufacturing leaders raised more than twenty years ago. The answer of course is yes! "Toyota did it," they said, "*but* they build cars; we build computers." Or "Yes, *but* we design and make information systems." Or "Yes, *but* we ____" (fill in the blank). And, yes, that is particularly the case in government: where the retort is "Yes, but we don't make widgets…We serve people, and people are unique and are not widgets!"

The fact that they all make different products is irrelevant. Operational Excellence, Lean (i.e., TPS), works for all of them, including government, because they all make use of processes to convert inputs into outputs for customers. And as we've discovered, it does not matter that the transformation of the inputs varies. Why? Because all work is a process. The fact is, if other people can do it, then those who lead and work in government can, without a doubt, change as well. In a UK government office processing a large volume of standard documents, Lean (Operational Excellence) techniques achieved double-digit productivity gains.[10] There are also examples of successful starts here in the United States, though, as of this writing and to our knowledge yet, no complete makeovers. In the Maine Departments of Labor, Transportation, Health and Human Services, Finance and Administrative Services, and Public Safety and the Maine Bureaus of Motor Vehicles and Human Resources, more than 65 percent of the workforce of Maine state government had extensive success using *BTC* leadership and management approaches and tools. We discuss their results in Chapter 7. Why is it imperative that change is framed as a journey? Why not just name the change needed and make it happen? Many a leader has tried, and failed, when change did not include consideration of the *process* of change.

Linda Ackerman Anderson, cofounder and transformational change consultant of Being First, Inc. and organizational transformation, defines "the three most prevalent types of change occurring in an organization as *developmental change, transitional change, and transformational change.*"[11] Transformational change, the most difficult and complex of the three, "is the radical shift from one state of being to another, so significant that it requires a shift in culture, behavior, and mindset to implement successfully and sustain over time."[12]

---

10 Nina Bhatia and John Drew, "Applying Lean Production to the Public Sector," *McKinsey Quarterly Review* (2006).

11 Dean Anderson and Linda A. Anderson, *Beyond Change Management: Advanced Strategies for Today's Transformational Leaders* (Jossey-Bass/Pfeiffer, 2011), 31.

12 Ibid., 39.

Mindset

Mindset is defined as "our fundamental assumptions about reality and our core beliefs about self, others, and life in general—i.e. our mental models. (Our) mindset is comprised of several independent variables that collectively work together as one integrated system to form our worldview."[13] To truly change our mindset, we must first expose ourselves to new knowledge while simultaneously applying new ideas to our work and acquiring experiential knowledge. Transformational change also requires a shift in a leader's mindset. They must be convinced that changes are needed and will make a difference in the organization. This means that concrete results must be available for them to see within their own organization. A field trip to a "Lean" plant, for example, may be a good start, but what happens within their own organization is what matters most.

To better ensure success with *BTC*, adapted from Flinchbaugh and Carlino's "A Thousand-Step Journey: The Five Phases of the *Lean* Transformation Roadmap,"[14] the minimal requirements for this transformation are as follows:

- There must be commitment and direct involvement among the top priorities of the top of the house of the organization, enterprise, or institution. In state government, the top of the house must include the commissioner of the agency in question, should include bipartisan championship in the legislature, the governor with formal legislative support, or a deputy commissioner or division director of a stand-alone "division."
- There must be an identifiable burning issue (i.e., a "burning platform" or a "must-be-solved pervasive problem" present.
- The aims of the initiative and the aim of the work unit are one and the same.
- There is leadership commitment and active participation brought ever together with urgency.
- Necessary resources are made available. Initially, some external help will also be beneficial. However, the initiative should focus on building internal qualified resources.
- Measurement and evaluation must be insisted upon—if the transformation can't be measured, the system can't be changed.
- Participants must consistently honor the mandates of the new way of doing business. If not, then the current culture or "current reality" will try to maintain itself.

---

13 Ibid., 80.

14 Adapted from Jamie Flinchbaugh and Andy Carlino. *The Second Hitchhiker's Guide to Lean: Lessons from the Road.* (Dearborn, Michigan: Society of Manufacturing Engineers, 2006).

- No “project-size” initiatives should be attempted. The change must be sweeping and fundamental.

When that occurs, the change will drive support for a cultural shift throughout the organization.

The transformation must come from leadership.
—W. Edwards Deming

CHAPTER 2: GETTING STARTED

The Historical Context

In Maine state government, the most comparable initiative prior to Bend the Curve was Total Quality Management, which by and large failed to permanently transform government operations. TQM was implemented with a significant top-down approach. The state workforce was told to eliminate waste but without a rigorous method to identify and eliminate waste. Its approach solved problems with a limited TQM toolbox focusing on budgetary/financial themes with the expectation that doing this would improve processes and produce better outcomes. While there were a structure and improvement goals, there was no systematic process or methodology for problem-solving and decision-making. Some departments had successful outcomes, while others were limited, but it did overall raise the expectations of employees by giving some an opportunity to participate in improvement efforts. It also had strong executive leadership and support from the chief executive (the governor), less so at the midlevel manager position where it was seen as a threat to their authority. Unfortunately, the governor attempted to initiate TQM in the last two years of his second term, which, given the size and scope of the effort, severely limited the available time to fully implement it. When the next administration came in, TQM was not a top priority initiative; oversight was moved from the governor's office to a Labor-Management Committee, and without the governor's direct involvement, momentum waned, and it was abandoned within the first two years of the new administration. This led to considerable disappointment for state employees given the high expectations that were set in the previous administration, particularly around their participation in problem-solving and improvement activities. Sadly, this gave rise to enduring cynicism in the workforce about any change/improvement effort, particularly if it smacked of quality improvement.

Challenges in Adapting Lean in Government

When Maine's Lean initiatives started, Bend the Curve found itself in an essentially foreign land because we discovered that it had to extensively adapt and translate the manufacturing-based concepts; language; methodologies like value stream mapping (VSM), rapid improvement (*kaizen*), variation, et cetera; and tools like Plan Do Check Act, Five Whys, 5S, et cetera to a government environment. At this time, in 2004, examples of Lean in government were few, and as noted before, there was considerable resistance and cynicism in the state's workforce. Bend the Curve had to adapt time-tested Lean principles and methods from the manufacturing sector and combine them with an array of continuous-improvement and TQM approaches to create a customized improvement process for government that sought to fundamentally alter the culture and work of the state of Maine. Specifically designed and adapted for government services, *BTC* developed system strategies, infrastructure, methodologies, and intervention tools for developing and supporting *internal* volunteer "consultant" capacity (to be called continuous improvement practitioners, CIPs) to assist government staff, clients, and contracted providers/partners to understand Lean and continuous improvement in order to transform government processes, increase value, and lower costs.

Bend the Curve sought to address the following challenges:

- **Changing Service Demands and Resource Levels**. Increasing and more complex service demands and decreasing resources demand greater governmental efficiencies and effectiveness. As economic conditions deteriorated, Maine faced an increasing rise in unemployment and demand for public benefits and services. The state also held one of the worst ratings for companies to do business in, as well as one of the highest tax burdens in the country. Politically, simply raising taxes was not a viable option.
- **Transformation of a Command and Control Culture**. Historically, government has supported a culture and structure that is generally hierarchical—not responsibility based—promoting control, blame/shame dynamics, power, privilege, and organizational silos. The state must also deal with issues associated with bureaucracy, which may often be entrenched and include an aging workforce, frequent management turnover, and two strong labor unions that needed to see the benefit of this type of change.

- **Perception of Government.** Citizens' perception has been that government is wasteful, with confidence in it eroding steadily over time. Maine was experiencing the same general malaise that most of the county was in with respect to the growth of government and its increasing cost and inability to deliver services in an efficient and effective manner.

Downsizing: A Fertile Ground?

The gubernatorial election in Maine takes place every four years. The 2004 election saw a new democratic governor facing significant budget deficits and a citizenry increasingly hostile to its tax burden and the overall economic direction in which the state was heading. To address these concerns, the new administration initiated a major reorganization effort in order to reduce costs by downsizing government. The planning for this reorganization included as one of its goals the merger of two of the largest state departments, the Department of Human Services and the Department of Behavioral and Developmental Services, BDS (formerly the Department of Mental Health, Mental Retardation, and Substance Abuse Services), into a new department called the Department of Health and Human Services (DHHS). In addition to their reorganization efforts, all the state departments were asked to reduce their budgets derived mostly from reducing workforce numbers.

Lean Start-Up

Faced with substantial, ongoing cuts in state and federal funds, the Maine Department of Labor (MDOL) set as a goal saving money through attrition rather than layoffs and doing its work radically differently and better. It was within the context of this transition to a smaller and more efficient government that the seeds of Maine's Lean initiative, Bend the Curve, were sown on ground that proved to be fertile for both the Maine Department of Labor (+600 employees) and the newly merged Department of Health and Human Services (+3800 employees). At the time and unknown to each other, Arthur Davis, then director of operations of MDOL and Walter Lowell, then director of information services of DHHS, having previous experience in TQM and knowledge of Lean/continuous quality improvement, initiated separate Lean efforts in 2004. Later that year, they began their collaborative discussions and work to found Maine's innovative, interdepartmental *BTC* program with the goal of applying Lean principles and methods to government operations.

The Challenges

BTC faced three major challenges: (1) Lean was thought to be exclusively a manufacturing approach; (2) civil servants were unaccustomed to viewing themselves in terms of customer, process, supplier, and production dynamics; and (3) a previous history of "failed" quality improvement initiatives.

MDOL's Challenge: The MDOL was faced with saving $9 million in its biennial budget. A typical response to meeting this target was laying off state employees since they represented the biggest cost center in the budget, but Arthur Davis's previous work with Digital Equipment Corporation (DEC) enabled him to see a different approach. MDOL began its Lean initiative when Arthur, as director of operations, convinced his commissioner, Laura Fortman, there was a better way to achieve savings without the painful cost of layoffs, which are so demoralizing to staff and the organization. Together, Arthur and his commissioner named this effort Bend the Curve to emphasize the idea of meeting demand for departmental services without the typical corresponding increase in money and other resources. When expenses overtake the funds generated (the revenue curve), bending the expense curve so that it matches the funds curve either becomes necessary; else one must find more funds to match the expense curve. This is generally not a good option in government since more funds are found primarily by increased taxation. Readers are reminded that the MDOL is in place to provide a safety net for workers. A major purpose of the safety is to provide a temporary "net" for unemployed workers. Given that that

> In his tenure at Digital Equipment Company (DEC), Arthur had the opportunity to go to Japan and study the revolutionary business system that Toyota was using to effectively compete with American automakers. What he saw was the Toyota Production System, which later became known as Lean, in action. Arthur says he returned from Japan a changed man.

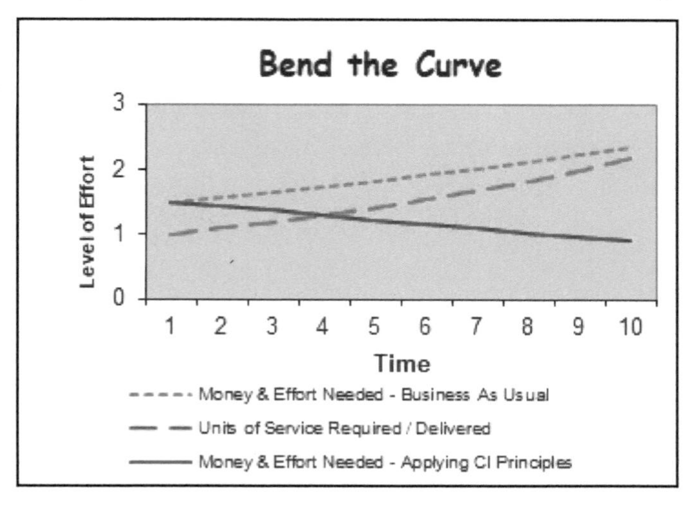

is our charter, it would be exceedingly difficult/more likely impossible to find the necessary funds to cover any shortfall.

By using Lean, we sought to "bend the cost curve"—of business as usual—by improving government processes, eliminating waste, and changing the fundamental nature of how one does and thinks about work (i.e., doing more and better with less). Therefore, early in the process it was determined that the MDOL would actively pursue getting other agencies within the state government system to participate in Bend the Curve.

DHHS's Challenge: Across town Walter Lowell was faced with a different challenge. The chair of the reorganization committee for a proposed new DHHS was appointed as the new commissioner for DHHS. The commissioner had worked in state government years before when it adopted Total Quality Management and remembered its value in managing his organization. In the new DHHS, he wanted to transform the culture to one represented by the best practices of TQM, but Lean was unknown to him.

At the time Walter, as the director of information services, was also the project director for the development of the soon-to-be-merged BDS's first enterprise-wide web information system. Prior to this position he was director of quality assurance at Maine's largest state psychiatric hospital and was deeply involved in TQM efforts in the hospital and the state. Already interested in Lean, in the summer of 2004, he received an invitation to attend a presentation on Lean and 5S to be held at a large Maine manufacturing company. The invitation captured his interest, and he recruited a small team of equally interested employees. They spent an evening learning how the company made huge improvements in workflow and waste reduction using 5S and how this tool along with other Lean tools were transforming how this and other local businesses did their work. Walter and the group returned inspired by the possibilities of Lean thinking and what it could bring to government operations. Based on his reading of Pascal Dennis's book *Lean Simplified* cover to cover, he began holding afternoon classes for his staff on what he was learning and how it could be applied to his department's work.

A Lucky Break: One of Walter's former colleagues who was working with the new commissioner of DHHS asked to attend the class, and what she heard inspired her to report to the commissioner about the possibilities of using Lean as a tool to develop the culture the commissioner was seeking and to arrange a meeting of the two men. It did not take long for the commissioner to realize that Lean was the culture he wanted to develop in the new DHHS. Given the merger challenges, the large size of the DHHS department, its geographic spread, and the work that needed to be done to implement Lean, Walter proposed the creation of an Office of Lean Management, reporting directly to the commissioner; to lead the effort to implement Lean in the new DHHS. The commissioner agreed to establish two full-time staff assigned to the office. This was, notably, perhaps one of the first such offices of Lean management to be established in a state government.

The MDOL and DHHS Lean Meeting: At this time, Walter heard about the Bend the Curve initiative that Arthur was starting to implement at the Maine Department of Labor. They met and shared their interest and where each was in his effort to introduce Lean. It was agreed that even though each department had slightly different transformational goals for initiating Lean—MDOL was seeking to balance its budget with minimum disruption of its workforce and services while DHHS was seeking to transition two separate departments, BHS and DHS, into one efficient and effective organization—both departments had similar goals regarding improving the productivity of their respective workforces by using Lean principles and methods and, therefore, would benefit from each other's work.

Arthur had one big advantage: his commissioner would eventually allocate a three-year budget of $765,000 dollars to support MDOL's *BTC* effort. Arthur hired two external consultants to get started; an organization development specialist and a specialist in Lean operations. Walter's advantage was working in the state's largest department having the largest percentage of state employees, and thus a greater potential impact on overall state operations, and also employees assigned to be fully dedicated to implementing Lean in DHHS. In addition, he was given a dedicated budget line for two positions (Full Time Equivalents (FTEs) and expenses and space set aside for Lean activities—which became known as the Lean Lab discussed in Chapter 5.

MDOL Launch Strategy: Arthur, along with the consultants, developed an implementation strategy that began with making MDOL staff aware of the *BTC* initiative and demonstrating to staff how Lean tools could be used to effectively improve services. A longer-term goal was to train internal Lean consultants, called continuous improvement practitioners (CIPs), to (1) embed a skilled cadre of staff able to teach, mentor, and lead Lean improvement efforts and (2) develop Lean practitioner training modules for ongoing training of CIPs to remove the need for external consultants.

The Budget: As the MDOL *BTC* program designer, Arthur was asked to create the budget. He calculated that it would cost the MDOL roughly $265,000 in the first year to accomplish what was in the plan. The budget was broken into two segments. Arthur knew that he did not want to create a request for proposal (RFP) and go to the open market for consultants; it would be too time consuming, and, at the time, there were not enough skilled Lean consultants. Therefore, he wrote a sole-source contract. The justification: we needed consultants who had demonstrated their ability to make use of a private sector manufacturing tool in a public sector transactional environment.

The Initial MDOL Budget

1. $210,000: Consulting fees for two consultants at $2900 per day
2. $50,000: "Things and stuff" to minimize the frequency of participants getting up and leaving and for off-site learning for students, break and lunch provisions, recognition rewards, et cetera
3. $0: The cost of leaders, managers, and value "stream teams" and observers' participation in improvement events and workshops.

"This is the Work": Arthur was "encouraged" by the bureau directors to include the cost of workers, supervisors, managers, themselves, the commissioner, et cetera when participating in process improvement work. By encouraged, he means they vigorously fought tooth and nail to have their participation included in the *BTC* budget as a "cost." Their logic went something like this: "Arthur, the people you're taking away to do *BTC* process improvement work have important jobs and/or critical projects. They do not have time to do "your *BTC* projects."

Arthur's protest was, "This is the work!" but they would have none of that. So rather than just glibly saying "This is the work," Arthur began to play back to them the logic of their argument, which was: "You (bureau/division director) would rather continue to have employees produce poor quality work, late delivery, or duplicates and continue to waste more money—thus, making life more challenging for you (bureau/division director)? Or would you rather free them up for three days (the proposed time it takes to conduct a value stream map) and have them learn how to do their work right the first time and not only save money but make customers happy also?" At first blush, their argument seemed reasonable. However, over time, Arthur was able to persuade them that the people who did the work were the most logical people to improve the work. In time and with positive results, the leaders saw Arthur's argument as compelling.

The overall cost of the Bend the Curve program is illustrated below; the overall cost of *BTC* was on the order of $765,000 over a three-year period.

Appendix G displays the strategy developed to implement Bend the Curve for MDOL.

External Consulting Costs for MDOL[1]

	Budget			**Savings**		
	Year	**Number of Consultants**	**Total Costs**	**Identified Savings**	**Cost to Savings Ratio**	**Potential Savings**
	1	**2**	**265,000**	**-**	**-**	**NA**
	2	**2**	**300,000**	**12,000,000**	**1 to 8**	**NA**
	3	**1.5**	**200,000**	**NA**	**1 to 26**	**$23,468,947**
TOTAL	**3**	**5.5**	**$765,000**	**$12,000,000**		**$23,468,947**

Given state budget constraints at the time, *BTC* operated with minimal expenditures beyond essential, ongoing operational costs (personnel, physical plant, phones, supplies, et cetera). *BTC* addressed budget constraints by forming collaborative relationships with other departments (MDOL and DHHS) and sharing resources. Some *BTC* Lean learning "events" were self-supporting and provided at cost to the participants. Other events were free.

BTC **Personnel:**

3.2 FTE's—Total fully burdened annual cost: $316,911

1.0 FTE in MDOL ($113,492: 5 percent state, 10 percent special state revenues, and 85 percent federally funded)

0.2 FTE MDOL planning member ($17,621: 95 percent state, 5 percent federally funded)

2.0 FTE in DHHS ($102,269 and $83,529 state funded).

Eighteen active "volunteer" CIPs, across several departments, with varying amounts of their time devoted to *BTC* initiatives, depending on demand and schedules. On average, 12.5 percent of their work time (the rough equivalent of 2.25 FTEs) at an average fully burdened cost of $83,500/year = $10,500. The total cost: $189,000.

The *BTC* **Model:** The basic model for Bend the Curve and its goals are set forth below:

1. Transformation of a Manufacturing Model to Government: Translating Lean principles, methodology, and tools to a government environment, based on the principles of continuous improvement and respect for people.
2. Internal Capacity: Rather than relying on external consultants, *BTC* focuses on training an internal "volunteer" interdepartmental capacity of continuous improvement practitioners (CIPs) in Lean and continuous improvement principles and methods.
3. Continuous Development: To be a CIP is a developmental journey. *BTC* structure provides required and other special trainings/workshops, monthly day-long clinicals, study missions, and a certification process.
4. Interdepartmental Commitment: A natural consequence of learning and practicing Lean concepts. *BTC* and its CIPs understand that the ability to improve the work is based on cross-functionality.
5. Introduction of Kaizen and Value Stream Mapping Approaches to Government: *BTC's* work and strategy are based on an integrated, team-oriented approach.
6. Holistic Implementation Model: Development of an implementation strategy that brings together CI/Lean principles, practices, knowledge, and strategies. This recognizes that it is as much about the hearts and minds of individuals as it is their technical skills and knowledge.

Changes in Practice:

1. Demands an integrated, standardized approach to improving government work, from all involved with and/or benefiting from the work, regardless of "ownership."
2. Develops a respected, problem-solving, critical-thinking workforce at all levels.
3. Provides staff with a government/service-oriented improvement approach, methods, and tools, making them accessible and easy to use.

First Steps: One of MDOL's first efforts was to begin holding Lean Awareness sessions with its staff around the state. These sessions were designed to inform staff about the basic strategy of using Lean methods and principles to meet the governor's budget goals without laying off staff. The initial five goals of the *BTC* were as follows:

1. Provide the same or better service.
2. Shift the work of the department to match customer expectations and needs.

3. Achieve efficiencies by fundamentally changing how work gets done.
4. Improve interdepartmental collaboration and service integration.
5. Decrease expenditures by $9 million and significantly reduce staffing levels over three years while minimizing layoffs.

One expected outcome from these sessions was for managers and staff to identify problems that would be demonstration projects and the focus of Lean improvement efforts. The initial "rollout" stated that within two months many of the MDOL staff would have an opportunity to experience the uses of "lean through demonstration projects." We wanted to use value stream mapping as a demonstration tool. A value stream mapping team consists of around eight to twelve people. The people who make up a value stream team are the employees who work on the value stream (i.e., the process) and one person who is somewhat unfamiliar with the process. The thinking being that the person unfamiliar with the process is likely to ask the uninformed question. Our first demonstration project would be a set of projects done at a facility that could accommodate teams of eight to ten people. The event had seven or eight teams all doing process improvement work simultaneously. The approach that the MDOL used is a standard change management method that entails starting with the whole or at least a significant number in the organization (versus starting small). The idea is to use methods that get everyone in the system included in making change a reality.

This led to the identification of eighteen improvement projects. To meet this demand, Arthur recruited ten additional state volunteers to help facilitate these project teams (Walter was one of the volunteers). All the volunteers had prior experience in improvement work or group/team facilitation. To standardize the work that this training cadre was about to embark upon, Arthur and the two consultants led a day-long training workshop for them on a standardized value stream mapping approach.

In the fall of 2004, *all* eighteen improvement project teams, along with the consultants and volunteer facilitators, were brought together at an external work site for a day-long "blitz" on Lean methods for beginning improvement work on their respective identified problems. Each team was assigned one of these trained facilitators, who led them through a value stream mapping process supervised by the Organizational Development consultants and Lean operations consultant. At the end of the day, all eighteen teams had developed a map of their respective work processes along with recommended improvements.

Initial Lessons Learned: Several key lessons were learned from this effort. Since volunteers could not always be available, it was important to develop an internal capacity knowledgeable and skilled enough to facilitate improvement teams. It was also important to begin and continue to develop and standardize the Lean improvement approaches to value stream mapping and *kaizen* in government.

The improvement teams themselves included people of different ages, tenure of service in state government, and education. Most had little to no experience in improvement work although a few did remember TQM, which occurred the decade before. The ideas of workflow, process, value and nonvalue-added time, and lead time and the concept of waste were new to almost all of them. It was clear that building competent internal capacity for *BTC* would require deliberate, concerted planning and effort. The staff who wanted to become continuous improvement practitioners (CIPs) would need substantial training. Without CIPs in place, continuing to hire consultants would be costly and thus prohibitive for most state departments. A key strategic goal for *BTC* became the development of CIPs who would be able to provide ongoing support to *BTC* and the state improvement efforts. This required the design, development, and implementation of an ongoing training and support program that could provide this resource. The training developed was called the development of practitioners training program and is discussed in the next chapter.

You cannot achieve an aim unless you have a method.
—W. Edwards Deming

CHAPTER 3: DEVELOPING CONTINUOUS IMPROVEMENT PRACTITIONERS

While there was some senior management support from the outset, we realized that neither of the authors had the experience and skill necessary to implement a comprehensive Lean program in our respective departments. This was brought home to us when we did the offsite blitz improvement event (discussed above) for MDOL with the eighteen teams. Arthur had recruited volunteers for a few days to assist in facilitating these sessions, but clearly, we could not rely on them to be available to drive a Lean program forward. The lesson was clear: we needed a strategy to develop an internal Lean practitioner capacity. This would prove a considerable challenge in identifying individuals willing and able to lead improvement teams, developing a training program and standardizing materials that would guide their work, building a supporting infrastructure and assuring that the same message would be delivered to improvement teams throughout state government.

The MDOL's external *BTC* consultants, skilled in organizational development and Lean operations, were set to work to design a training program that would enable us to train state employees in Lean principles and methods, with a skill set that would enable them to facilitate improvement teams. This meant developing a training program for state staff that had very little experience in Lean and continuous improvement, system change methods, or even group facilitation. In addition, staff had to be brought up to speed very quickly, enabling them to begin process improvement work immediately after the training. This meant standardized training guides had to be developed to assist them in this work.

Development of Practitioners: In January of 2005, the first of what would become eight development of practitioners (DOP) introductory trainings and two enhanced trainings was launched. The introductory DOP was designed as a week-long training that ran from 7:30 a.m. to 5:00 p.m. with breakfast, snacks, coffee and lunch provided each day by a caterer. This was an unusual design for state government since very few training programs were this long and provided meals. The rationale for the onsite food was to assure that the participants remained on site and did not have to go out for lunch and had energy-boosting snacks, et cetera. Participant departments were charged a fee to participate in the DOP. The initial fee was $1,700 per trainee and covered the cost of the consultants, food, and all materials. The price was reduced considerably once state staff took over the training; while state staff were also part of the training team, it was approximately two years before *BTC* state staff felt confident enough to design and deliver the training entirely without external consultants.

This training was opened to any staff in state government who were interested and could convince their supervisors to allow them to spend a week away from their primary work duties. Initially, applicants were screened by the two MDOL consultants. The screening was intended to assure that the first round of trainees (1) knew what they were getting into, (2) had the support and commitment of their supervisors for ongoing participation, and (3) had some experience with leading groups. For this first DOP, twenty-three state employees from a variety of different departments attended the DOP training.

The CIP Model: Continuous improvement practitioners were to be change agents providing leadership and expertise as their respective departments moved forward with implementing Lean. In this role, practitioners would do the following:

- Facilitate groups engaged in various system/process improvement activities
- Coach managers/sponsors and team leaders about appropriate methodology/tool selection
- Coach managers/sponsors and team leaders about implementation and oversight strategies
- Ensure appropriate documentation
- Support measurement and reporting of results
- Provide broad *BTC*/Lean expertise and consultation

Continuous improvement practitioners were also expected to be engaged in continuous learning and participate in ongoing *BTC* development to teach and to implement what they had learned to their respective departmental staff.

We acknowledged that one week of classroom training (forty hours) could not possibly provide all the necessary skills, experience, and knowledge needed for them to be successful. They were also expected to deepen and broaden their knowledge and understanding of the concepts being learned, teach by modeling new behaviors, and influence their work culture. This set the bar very high for those staff wanting to participate as CIPs in *BTC*. The ideal qualifications for those seeking to participate in the *BTC* program are listed below.

CIP Qualifications and Abilities.

Listed below are the expectations for CIP participation in *BTC*:

- They are enthusiastic about the *BTC*/Lean principles, methods, techniques, and approach and have an ability, willingness, and enthusiasm for becoming a formal change agent in the *BTC* initiative.
- They can make the mandatory time commitment *and* participate fully:
    - At least a two-year commitment
    - A minimum of thirty-six days a year for *BTC*/Lean activities, including those activities listed *above.*
- They have full and strong management and supervisory support for doing this state of Maine and department-wide work.
- They are willing and eager to learn, internalize, and apply new and sometimes challenging ideas and skills.
- They can give *and* receive feedback.
- They can demonstrate active listening skills.
- They have good written and oral communication skills.
- They can demonstrate a preference and willingness to use facts, or to learn to use facts, metrics, observations, and analysis versus guesses, assumptions, or expedient inferences/conclusions to prove a point.

Miller, Ken, *We Don't Make Widgets*, Governing Management Series, 2006.

Flinchbaugh, Jamie and Andy Carlino, *The Hitchhiker's Guide to Lean*, Society of Manufacturing Engineers, 2006.

Womack, James and Daniel Jones, *Lean Thinking*, Free Press: New York, 2003.

Schwarz, Roger, *The Skilled Facilitator*, 2002.

- They are comfortable with and have the ability (to learn) to lead/work effectively with diverse groups, preferably with some experience in working with groups.
- They accept the concept that development of *self* is core to leadership competency.

Materials and methods: Students attending the DOP were each given a development of practitioner workbook with training materials for each day of the week. This workbook contained training modules designed to teach each of the five competencies discussed below, using adult learning approaches. Each student was also given a set of reference books on Lean and facilitation as well as a journal to record their experiences and lessons learned for the week. A list of the books appears in the sidebar.

The DOP training strategy was organized for adult learners which alternated between in-class instruction, small and large group activities, and practical hands-on experiences and simulations to reinforce the classroom lessons. This was a "learn and do" approach and would be a crucial part of all subsequent improvement work and training. Figure 3.1 displays a typical DOP weekly schedule.

The Five Competencies

The DOP sought to develop five competencies deemed necessary for the CIPs to be successful. These are (1) self, (2) group, (3) change, (4) process, and (5) Lean as depicted below.

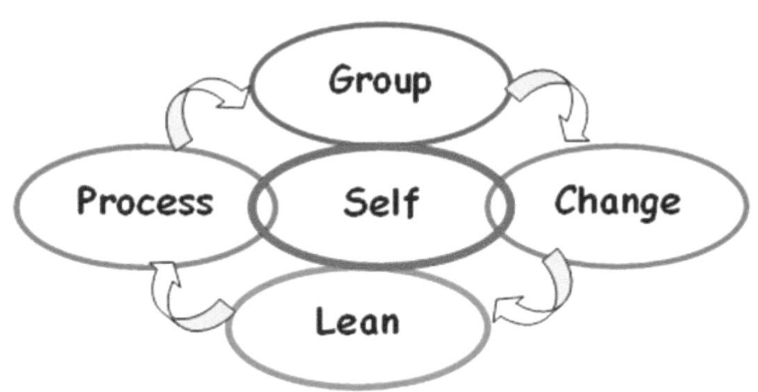

Self: "Use of self refers to how one acts upon one's observations, feelings, values, etc., in order to affect a person or system. It involves having an impact, giving of yourself, providing a force not presently operating in the system, and putting yourself on the line."[15] The notion of self as an instrument of change can be

15

understood as an essential component in the practitioner's ability to successfully enter into relationships, navigate the "helping" process, and fill a wide range of roles. And at the end of the day, "we have only ourselves to use as instruments as we engage in leading others. Therefore, we need constantly to know ourselves better."[16] Moreover, as we've learned, cultural change begins with behavioral change of self.

Group: Facilitating group process is the reasoned and intentioned intervention, on the part of the CIP, into the ongoing events and dynamics of a group with the purpose of helping that group attain its stated end more effectively.[17] To do this well, it is necessary to know enough theory, to understand relevant concepts such as stages of group and individual development. And it is necessary to be skilled enough to ask the right questions, present the right model, and stop or encourage the activity, et cetera. And it is critical that the practitioners be able to understand and be in control of their own beliefs, values, and needs sufficiently to act (or not act) in ways that are appropriate and relevant to the group being facilitated.

Change: As change agents, the CIP must have knowledge of the change process, kinds of change, and associated dynamics. In tandem, the change agent must have a framework of understanding and working with resistance. There are a wide variety of normal, legitimate bases of questioning, including "resisting" the pushes toward change. Effective facilitators of change—leaders, managers, change agents, practitioners—can use a variety of techniques of promoting support and collaboration in change efforts—if they can erase the negative meanings often associated with "resistance." One measure of the importance of a change effort is the degree of resistance that it generates. It is important to understand that resistance is energy that can transform into a positive force for improvement.

Process: All work is a process. Having a process mindset—knowing that all work is a process of inputs, transformation, and outputs—is sometimes referred to as systems thinking. Developing a process mindset is about "imprinting" the notion of "process" so that it is an automatic filter through which one views reality. It means *seeing* systems as a collection of processes. This perspective requires an understanding of the structure, functions, and dynamics of organizations and the principles of systems thinking. CIPs must have a working knowledge of the concepts and tools necessary to understand and manage the critical interrelationships between the organization and the external environment, as well as between the different subsystems within the organization. Without a process mindset, the ability

16 Bob Tannenbaum, PhD, Senior Faculty, NTL Institute, 1999.

17 Reddy-Phillips, Consultants to Organizations, 1988.

to see the waste and the drive to improve are usually lacking or absent, leaving the customer with less-than-satisfying results.

Lean/Continuous Improvement: CIPs must possess a solid understanding of the basic principles, methods, and tools of Lean and an ability to implement them in order to drive improvements and show measurable results. We started with a deep understanding of the core concepts: value, value stream, flow, pull, and perfection in tandem with a profound understanding of process mindset. CIPs then progressed through the "House of Lean," starting with value stream mapping (VSM).

House of Lean Thinking[1]

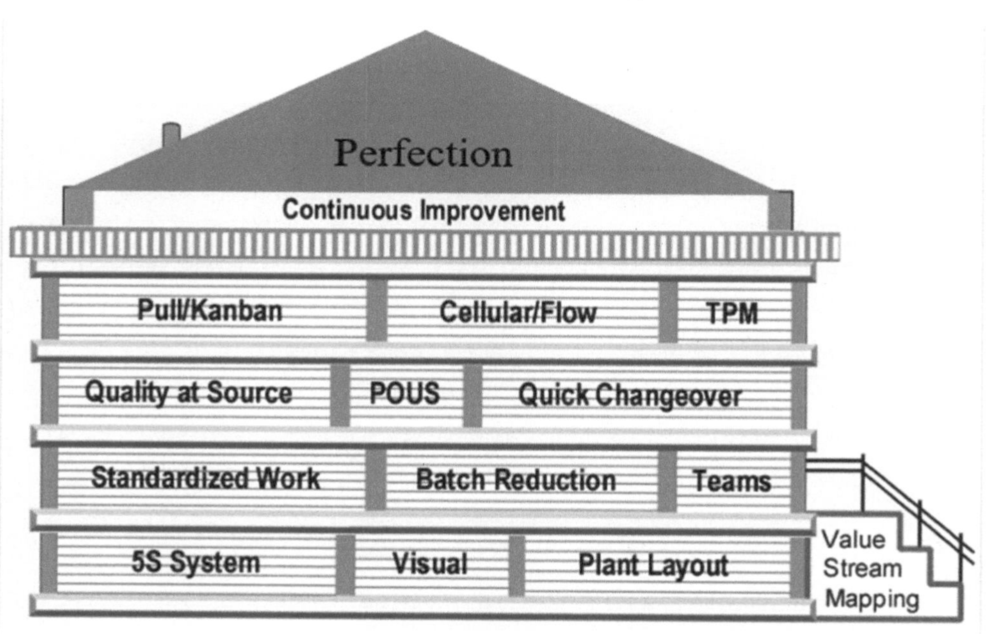

[1] From Maine Employees Manufacturing Partnership

The DOP Schedule: Each day of the week-long introductory DOP was focused on a particular theme:

Day 1, Developing a Process Mindset
Day 2, Making Work Visible
Day 3, Improving a Process
Day 4, Implementing a New Process
Day 5, Perfecting the Lean Process

Each day had modules that focused on a variety of specific topics designed to teach Lean principles and methods and continuous process improvement concepts, group facilitation skills, and Lean tools needed for the students to be successful in their work coaching and leading improvement efforts. The five competencies were emphasized where appropriate in each module and lesson taught. A major component of the DOP was a "simulation" used to represent a typical government service process, which served as a framework and foundation for key ideas throughout the whole week. The simulation was purposely designed to illustrate a current state that contained waste and dysfunctions. Concepts of waste, value, value stream, workflow, process improvement, and others were presented with reference to the simulation the students experienced. The simulation was used to teach the value stream mapping (VSM) process, which included mapping the current state, identifying process measures and waste, and identifying improvement opportunities. These were then used later in the week to create future state and improvement plans that were tested to see if the team's improvement ideas worked. The small simulations groups were used to provide opportunity for the trainees to practice facilitation skills, feedback, and leading and coaching teams plus provide an opportunity for them to use the concepts and Lean tools they were taught and TOOTs (Time Out Of Time) were used as feedback sessions.

Development of Continuous Improvement (CI) Practitioners1 : Agenda

Day 1- Monday	Day 2- Tuesday	Day 3- Wed.	Day 4- Thursday	Day 5- Friday
7:30 Gather, Breakfast 8:00 □Start-up □Community building □Contracting □Break □Simulation: *"Service Request"* □Tool Box – overview □Process mindset (1)	7:30 Gather, Breakfast 8:00 □Start-up □Check-in: Learning trios □VSM Start-up: Steps - Input, demo □Break □VSM Start-up continued - Practicum & Debrief □TOOT □VSM current state - Input □Worksheet: VS - NVA	7:30 Gather, Breakfast 8:00 □Start-up □Check-in □Current State: round 2 - Practicum & debrief □CS TOOT □Break □Flow: simulation & input □VSM future state - Input □Worksheet: Waste	7:30 Gather, Breakfast 8:00 □Start-up □Intervention Cycle □Learning groups □Measurement (2) □Documentation □Break □Kaizen - Input - Practicum & Debrief □Close practicum groups □Kaizen TOOT	7:30 Gather, Breakfast 8:00 □Start-up □VSM II - Set-up - Practice Day 1- Debrief □Break □VSM II continued - Practice Day 2 - Debrief - TOOT □Unfinished business
12:30 □Lunch	12:30 □Lunch	12:30 □Lunch	12:30 □Lunch	12:30 □Lunch
1:15 □Learning structures □Practitioner Roles □Tracking □Break □Chartering - Worksheet: 3-Way - Practice & Debrief □Check-out □Assignments 5:30 · Adjourn	1:15 □Set-up Task □VSM Current State - Practicum & debrief □TOOT □Break □Measurement (1) □Learning trios: Self □Check-out □Assignments 5:30 · Adjourn	1:15 □VSM Future State - Practicum & Debrief □Future State TOOT - Learning groups: data sheet questions □Break □Implementation □Parking lot: large group □Check-out □Assignments 5:30 · Adjourn	1:15 □Standardization, 5S's, 5Why's, visual controls □Process mindset (2) □Break □Set-up VSM II 3:30 Lessons Learned: CIP Round Table 5:00 · Adjourn 5:30 Group Dinner (Optional)	1:15 □BTC Jeopardy □Forward Planning □Development plans □Close learning trios □Closing ritual 4:00 · Adjourn

Figure 1

Design Notes: Each module in the DOP had specific design notes developed for the instructors that included overall goals and objectives for each module, new vocabulary and concepts that were being introduced, detailed notes on actual activities that were to be used, and concepts and questions for the students. The design notes showed the time, the content, any materials needed, and the individuals responsible for each module.

The idea behind the design notes concept was to standardize the presentations so that any member of the team instructing the class, if necessary, could step in and successfully teach the module/lesson. The design notes took a considerable amount of time to develop but enabled instructors to build on them and improve them, and as the DOP evolved, we learned what worked and what didn't. Each module duration and flow were timed to match the time allotted in the overall daily schedule for the day. Every module had a PowerPoint slide deck developed for students to follow along as the module progressed. The PowerPoint listed the flow of the module and major concepts and ideas to be presented. A typical design note for a module is displayed in appendix B.

Process measures: In mapping a process, we originally taught a standard set of measures for each step in the process. These initially were typical manufacturing metrics that we adopted to quantify a process and included lead time, cycle time, and so on. This original set of measures is set forth in Table 2. We found early on that these measures were confusing for our CIPs and improvement teams involved in mapping processes. In part, we felt this was due to several reasons: (1) failure of government employees to see their work as a process, (2) resistance to the idea "we don't make widgets here" and the idea that their work couldn't be measured in these terms (actually it was not unusual to hear that "their work could not be measured at all"),(3) the concept of value creation and waste were only vaguely understood going into process mapping work, and (4) collecting all these measures proved to be very time consuming.

As we moved forward with the DOPs and the improvement work, we discovered that collecting this detailed data at this point in implementing Lean was overkill and unnecessary to make progress. These measures for each step in the process were simplified to include the concepts of staff time (defined as value-added or hands-on time) and elapsed time (defined as the total amount of time it took to complete a task, which included waiting and other nonvalue-added activities), percent complete, percent value-added, and first pass yield. The modified data sheet is displayed in Table 3. DOP instructors taught the idea behind VSM was to identify and remove waste by making elapsed time and staff time as close as possible. These two measures allowed us to make progress and were readily understood by the improvement teams we were working with.

Table 2
BTC's First Attempt at VSM Data Sheets with Definitions

Name of the Step/Process:
Step Description: Description of what is included in the step; what is encompassed in it.
Special Considerations: Notations about special needs, such as training, limitations, licenses, certifications, et cetera.
Amount of Work Waiting for This Step: How many people or items are waiting. Shows backlogs, excess inventory, and bottlenecks.
Cycle Time (CT): The amount of time it takes to complete one step/item from the end of the previous step to the end of the current step. Includes changeover time, wait time, et cetera.
# of People: Required to do this step for this one item at the same time.
Staff Time (ST): Amount of staff time involved in this step for *all* staff involved—this is the time actually spent acting on, doing, changing, or working with a person or single item multiplied by the # of people doing this work. Includes time waiting if performing other work is unlikely.
Value-Added (VA) Percent: An estimate of the percentage of value-added time within the cycle time for the step. This is what the customer would be willing to pay for if given the choice.
Required Nonvalue-Added (RNVA) Percent: An estimate of nonvalue-added time that is required by law, rule, regulation, or other mandate.
Change Over Time (CO): The amount of time it takes to change over from the end of the previous step to the beginning of this step—such as logging into a computer application, getting records/forms, setting up for customer encounters, et cetera.
Uptime Percent (UT): The percentage of time a person, program, printer, copier, et cetera, is available compared to the time each is expected to be available/run. For example, the time a supervisor is available for signatures or the time a copier works and is available.
First Pass Yield Percent (FYP): The percentage of time that quality standards are met the *first* time through; the percentage of time the step is completed correctly *the first* time.
Notes: All *pertinent* ideas, assumptions, and information—any information about the process that is important and not captured in other data boxes.

Table 3
Revised VSM Data Sheets

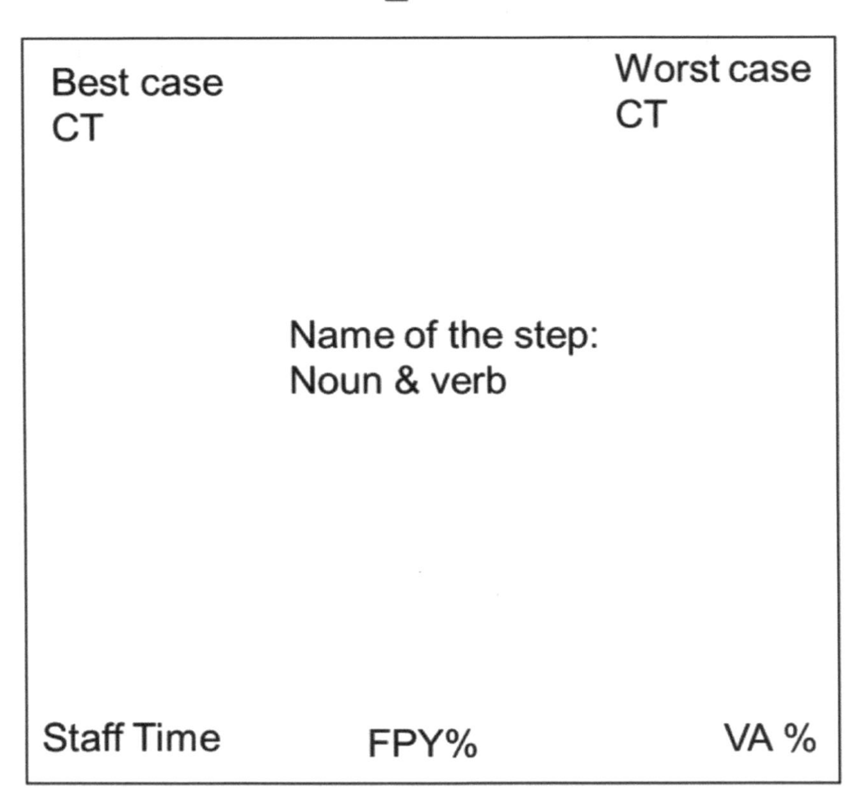

CT = Cycle Time
FPY% = Percent First Pass Yield
VA% = Percent Value Added

CIP Role and Expectations: CIPs were expected to be engaged in continuous learning and ongoing development and were expected to teach and implement what they had learned. Opportunities were provided for them to deepen and broaden their own knowledge and understanding of the concepts being learned, teach by modeling new behaviors, and influence the work culture to change through these processes. They were expected to coordinate, consult, and work closely with the Bend the Curve core team and other continuous improvement practitioners and might also be called upon to work with agencies and departments other than their own. CIPs were expected to influence overall change strategy by providing feedback and support to the *BTC* program team, the *BTC* steering committee, and their respective departmental senior leaderships.

Their overall responsibilities included attending and successfully completing, at a minimum, the following knowledge and skills development activities:

- Introductory five-day development of practitioner (DOP) training program
- Advanced/enhanced trainings as required, including the five-day enhanced development of practitioner training
- Regular continuous improvement practitioner clinical supervision team sessions at least one full day a month
- *BTC* development and organizational meetings as scheduled
- Bend the Curve special events, conventions, et cetera as held

CIPs were also expected to actively participate in and incorporate ongoing self-development, demonstrating willingness to learn, internalize, and apply new ideas and skills including:

- Successfully fulfilling continuous improvement practitioner certification requirements
- Demonstrating an ability and willingness to become a formal change agent
- Actively seeking feedback and integrating it in order to improve their skill level
- Engaging with peers to create a safe, supportive, and challenging learning environment
- Asking for help and being open to being coached
- Observing the process improvement work of others in order to learn and hone skills, including formal observation of at least two complete VSM processes and one kaizen
- Actively modeling desired behaviors of the new culture

In addition to participating fully in Bend the Curve/Lean activities, they facilitated and monitored system/process improvement event such as value stream mapping (VSM). This work included the following activities:

- Engage sponsors to effectively charter and implement process improvement and the work of the related teams
- Facilitate groups engaged in process improvement activities (value stream mapping, kaizen, problem-solving, 5S, and others), facilitating at least two complete VSM processes (VSM, kaizen, other rapid improvement interventions, et cetera) annually in either lead or co-lead roles
- Coach and/or lead others to develop recommendations and implement plans consistent with the *BTC* mission
- Complete, monitor/track, and evaluate, as needed, all continuous improvement practitioner work related to designated process improvement activities, such as implementation activities and performance measures

CIPs also provided comprehensive expertise, consultation, and other support regarding *BTC*/Lean as requested/required, modeling the *BTC*/Lean philosophy and approach:

- Demonstrating knowledge of *BTC* principles, methods, tools, and techniques
- Using facts, metrics, observations, and analysis versus guesses, assumptions, or expedient inferences/conclusions for planning, proof, and evaluation
- Providing feedback in service to continuous improvement
- Maintaining effective relationships with assigned customers

Evolution of DOP: The first DOP was designed and developed by the *BTC* external consultants, who developed their skills in the private sector. Neither had any extensive experience extensive experience working with Lean in a government setting. The role of the organizational development consultant was to mentor senior management at MDOL and provide skill training for staff in team building, group dynamics, and change initiatives. The Lean consultant's responsibilities were to provide leadership and skill building for state employees in Lean/continuous improvement methods and principles. These consultants, with Arthur Davis's guidance, designed and developed the first development of practitioner (DOP) training to develop a cadre of skilled state employees who would be able to lead teams in process improvement activities We quickly learned that a forty-hour week course was not enough to provide the skill level and knowledge needed. The following year a second advanced development of practitioner (DOP2) training was designed for attendees of the first two DOPs. DOP2 was designed to deepen CIP knowledge in group dynamics, team building, and Lean methods and tools. Over the next eight years *BTC* delivered eight DOP sessions and trained over seventy CIPs. One of the early goals of *BTC* was to have state employees assume responsibility for the evolving design and delivery of the DOPs. A core team consisting of Arthur and Walter and their respective staff fully assumed this responsibility in the third year of *BTC*. This team applied the same continuous improvement strategy that it taught, and the DOPs evolved considerably based on feedback from practicing CIPs and their customer base (i.e., state employee process improvement teams). Figure 1 displays the final DOP agenda and schedule.

Figure 1

Day 1: Monday	Day 2: Tuesday	Day 3: Wednesday	Day 4: Thursday	Day 5: Friday
Developing a Process Mindset	**Making Work Visible**	**Improving the Process**	**Implementing the New Process**	**Perfecting the Lean Process**
7:30 Gather, Breakfast **8:15 Welcome** · **Start-Up and Overview (45")** WEL/staff · **Learning Community and Learning Self (30")** (MAD) · ***Simulation** (WEL/Faculty) **(90")** · **Break** (10:30–10:45) · **Problem-Solving Approaches** (WEL/JK) **(30")** ·**Consulting Process (Entry and Contracting) (30")**	7:30 Gather, Breakfast **8:15 Start-Up (30")** · **Learning Community** WEL/faculty · **Lucy/Escalator Video (15")** (WEL) · **Five Lean Concepts and Flow (Lean Cards) Activity—Activities/Connections Flow (60")** (WEL/ASD) · **Break** · **System of Work (Process Mindset) (35")** (JK) · **Visualize the Process: Walk the Dog (40")** (MAD) · **Give and Receive Feedback (30")** (ASD/JLR)	7:30 Gather, Breakfast **8:15 Start-Up (30")** · **Learning Community** WEL/faculty · **Language of Waste + 3Bs + Miller's p. 142 + Value/Failure Demand (45")** (WEL) · **Module: Problem-Solving Tools (45")** (Faculty per tool) · **Break** (10:15–10:30) · **Applying Continuous Improvement Concepts (45")** (WEL/JLR) · **Mapping the Future State** (JK/MAD)	7:30 Gather, Breakfast **8:15 Start-Up (30")** · **Learning Community** WEL/faculty · **Development and Use of the Improvement Implementation Plan (90")** (JK/MAD) · **Break** · **Improved Simulation (90")** (WEL/Faculty)	7:30 Gather, Breakfast **8:15 Start-up (30")** · **Learning Community** WEL/faculty · **Change: Organizational and Individual (60")** (JK) · **Break** · **Change: Practice (60")** (WEL—IFW Case Study Example) ·**Improvement Project Integration**—Improvement Team Membership and Report Out **(45")** (JLR)

12:15 · Lunch	12:00 · Lunch	12:00 · Lunch	12:00 · Lunch	12:00 · Lunch
1:00 · **Measures: Mustang Exercise (20")** (JLR/WEL) · **Measurement:** What is it you need to know? **(45")** (JK) · **Types of Interventions and CIP Intervention Tools (60")** (MAD) · **Break** (3:05–3:20) · **Chartering (55")** MAD · **Improvement Project—Integration**—(WEL) **(30")** *Background/Customer/Product/Supplier* **5:00 · Adjourn**	**12:45** · **Mission Statement (30")** (MAD/JK) · **Process Analysis Matrix (30")** (JK) · **Intervention: Mapping the Current State (2'30")** (JK/MD) · **Break** (15") · **Intervention: Mapping Current State Continued** · **Improvement Project Integration**—Define the Problem—Measurement **(30")** (JLR) **5:00 · Adjourn**	**12:45** · **Mapping Future State** (cont'd.) (JK/MD) · **Break** (2:45–3:00) · **Measurement:** Continued **(30")** (JK) · **CS and FS Comparisons and Implications (45")** (WEL) · **Improvement Project Integration**—Outcomes/ Goals/ Targets and Measurement **(30")** (JK) **5:00 · Adjourn**	**12:45** · **5 Operational Principles (45")** (WEL/JK) · **Managing the IP (30")** (JK) · **Break** · **Intervention Follow-up and Role of the CIP (45")** (WEL) · **Standardization (45")** (JLR) · **Improvement Project Integration**—Proposed Intervention Type and Method **(30")** (MAD) **5:00 · Adjourn**	**12:45** · **Consulting Process:** Closure and Recontracting Exercise: Closing and Recontracting Learning Community **(30")** (MAD) · **Roles and Responsibility of CIPs (30")** (JK) · **CIP Development and Reentry Planning (45")** (JK/Faculty) · **Break** · **Summary, Next Steps, and Wrap-Up** (WEL/Faculty) **(45")** · **Closing Ceremony (30")** [Jeopardy] (WEL) **4:00 · Adjourn**

Figure 3 displays the organizational structure of *BTC*. Once the external consultants had finished, we established a four-person steering group that had primary responsibility for *BTC's* overall design and operation. This included 1) designing and delivering both of the week-long development of practitioners for the initial and advanced sessions; 2) designing and maintaining the CIP certification process; 3) establishing annual goals; 4) tracking improvement results; 5) designing monthly clinical sessions and 6) facilitating improvement sessions. Figure 4 displays the structures that were developed to support the CIPs in their practice. As the word got out about the training, we began accepting participants from partners outside of government as well. They were charged at the same fee level as state employees. Outside organizations included the state university, a local hospital, and a municipal government from New Hampshire. The total number of CIPs and the departments/organizations they represented are displayed in Table 3. Approximately seventy-eight people went through the introductory week-long DOP training to become CIPs. We found over the duration of *BTC* that we needed to offer the DOP at least once a year to continue to grow the number of CIP and because some trained staff left state government to work in the private sector or retired, and some were unable to continue as a CIP for a variety of reasons including job reassignment; lack of available to time to continue to participate; or inability to actually perform as a CIP. Throughout the duration of *BTC's* activities, there were approximately a dozen or so CIPs that were consistently available to lead improvement work.

As discussed above, the one week of training was not enough for participants to feel confident in leading improvement groups. We therefore set up a process where we linked new CIPs to experienced CIPs to mentor them through several improvement initiatives. This eventually led to a formal certification process, which we describe in chapter 5. Briefly, the process included observation and co-lead periods before they became a full lead, as well as a Lean knowledge test and the submission of a CIP portfolio. We also developed standard materials, methods, and processes to assist CIPs in their improvement work (described in chapter 4).

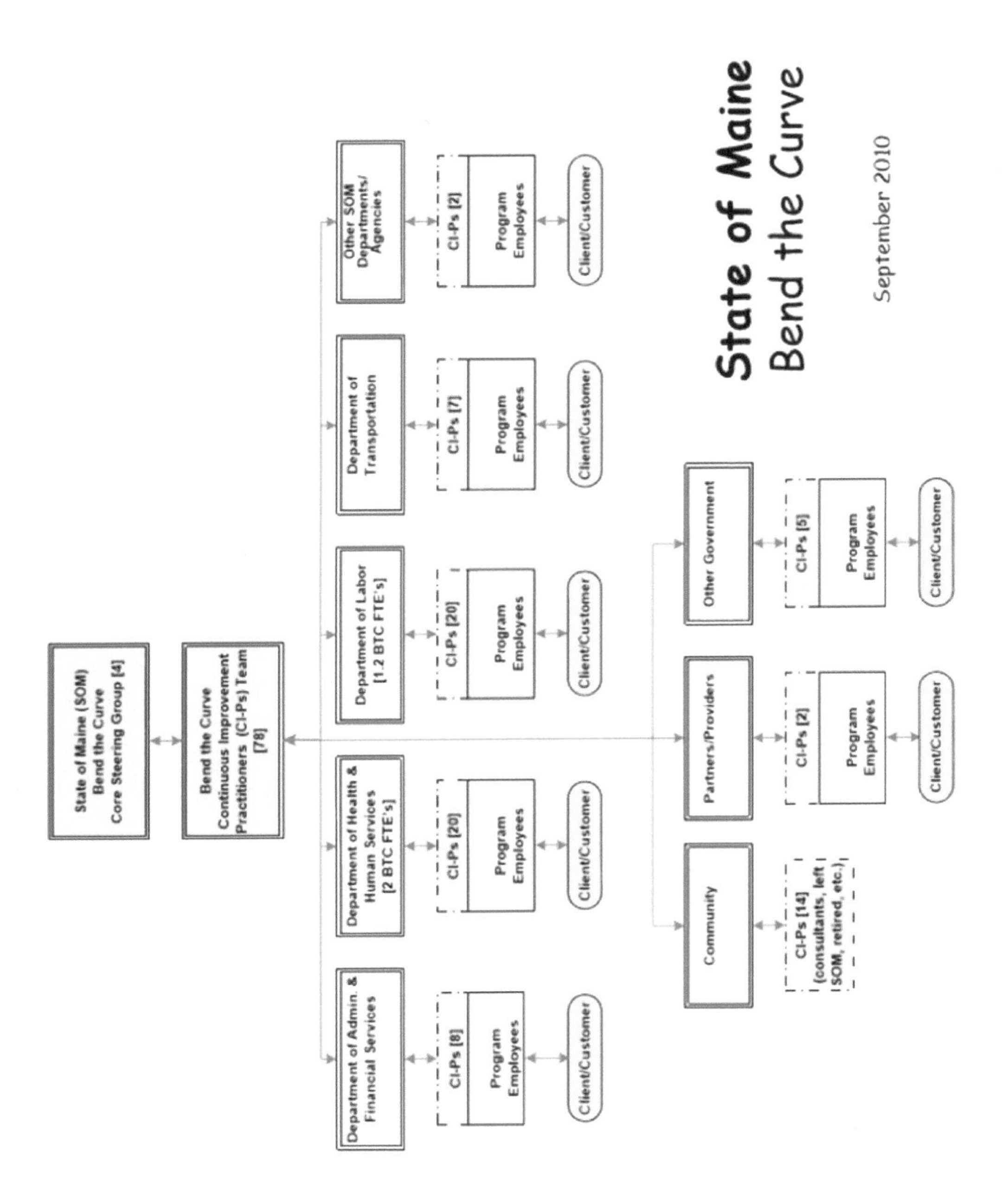
State of Maine
Bend the Curve
September 2010
State of Maine (SOM) Bend the Curve Core Steering Group [4]
Bend the Curve Continuous Improvement Practitioners (CI-Ps) Team [78]
Department of Admin. & Financial Services
Department of Health & Human Services [2 BTC FTE's]
Department of Labor [1.2 BTC FTE's]
Department of Transportation
Other SOM Departments/ Agencies
CI-Ps [8]
CI-Ps [20]
CI-Ps [20]
CI-Ps [7]
CI-Ps [2]
Program Employees
Client/Customer
Community
Partners/Providers
Other Government
CI-Ps [14] (consultants, left SOM, retired, etc.)
CI-Ps [2]
CI-Ps [5]

Figure 3

Table 3
Total CIPs Trained by *BTC*

Department/Organization	# CIPs Trained
Health and Human Services	**20**
Labor	**20**
Financial and Administrative Affairs	**8**
Transportation	**7**
Environmental Protection	**1**
Corrections	**1**
Local Hospital	**2**
Municipal Government	**5**
University/Community	**14**
Total Trained	**78**

We should work on our process, not the outcome of our processes.
—W. Edwards Deming

CHAPTER 4: CIP PRACTICE

The purpose of this chapter is to describe the set of standard Lean and continuous improvement processes and practices *BTC* customized for a government setting and how and why they were developed and improved. Initially, these were based on the Lean manufacturing model that we were originally taught. The general Lean principles of value, values stream, flow, pull, and perfection apply equally to government as they do to any business. Since value creation in government is mostly based on services, the idea of building a product or having customers was difficult for many CIPs and state employees to come to grips with. We realized the necessity of adapting the language of Lean to work in a government/service environment and set out to make these and other key Lean ideas more understandable to government workers.

One great insight came to us from Ken Miller's brilliant book *We Don't Make Widgets*. Miller addresses three myths common to government workers that are barriers to effective change: (1) governments don't make widgets (products); (2) governments don't have customers; and (3) they don't make a profit. We recognized that we were running directly into these barriers as well and began to address them directly by customizing our materials and methods to emphasize them throughout our DOP training and CIP improvement practices. Additionally, we invited Ken Miller to Maine several times to help us with these ideas and to provide additional training to the CIPs and more broadly to other state staff. These sessions proved to be immensely successful for us to move forward with *BTC* training and gave us confidence in the customization we were doing to improve *BTC's* standard improvement processes and methods.

Standard Processes: Standardization of process and procedures was heavily emphasized in our DOP training; however, we knew that most of the participants in a DOP training had very little knowledge about standardization, and some did not even feel it applied to their work, despite an intensive forty-hour training session. One of the tools and foundational principles of Lean is standardization, defined as: "Establishing high agreement of what and how."[18] We saw this as an opportunity to enable CIPs to begin the process of grasping standardization as a foundational principle of Lean by teaching them to develop, use and promote standard processes, procedures and protocols. These were standard written "guides" we called design notes that CIPs would create when they were doing improvement work with improvement teams. Design notes were standard protocols that could be customized for improvement events. They were taught in the DOP to follow them as closely as possible as appropriate and circumstances dictated.

> To the "process mindset novelist," standardization is translated as (1) a loss of freedom, creativity, and spontaneity, thus a waste of time and (2) after all, I'm providing "services" to a client, patient, et cetera (i.e., a human being) often under *very complex circumstances*, not run-of-the-mill "widgets." Standardization, contrary to this opinion, *saves time and exponentially provides for creativity, ingenuity, and far, far less stress, waste, and overall dissatisfaction.*

BTC's improvement intervention process followed a standard consulting model as diagramed in Figure 4.1. CIPs were encouraged to use this model in their improvement events. We developed standard written procedures around each item in this process, and these materials formed the basis of CIP practice and training. It is important to note here that after the first DOP training, CIPs were expected to begin to practice what they learned during their DOP week of training, using the materials they were given.

Follow the Process: The first round of CIPs jumped into improvement work not fully knowing how much they did not know nor how much more there was to know. In these early improvement efforts with state improvement teams, we learned as we did the work and made a lot of mistakes along the way but recognized that following a standard process gave us a very high probability of achieving success with the improvement teams we were working with

18 Jamie Flinchbaugh and Andy Carlino, *The Hitchhiker's Guide to Lean: Lessons from the Road* (Dearborn, Michigan: Society for Manufacturing Engineers, 2006).

and enabled us to continuously improve our materials. So much so that "follow the process" became a mantra with CIPs. We knew there was much to improve upon, but the standardized Lean methods and principles worked and made sense to state workers and gave them the confidence and support they needed to move forward.

Standard CIP Consulting Process: The standardized *BTC* consulting process is depicted in Figure 4.1. We would begin an internal consult after receiving a request from a department manager who had a problem that s/he wanted to "fix" using Lean. These requests were generally received over the phone.

Figure 4.1

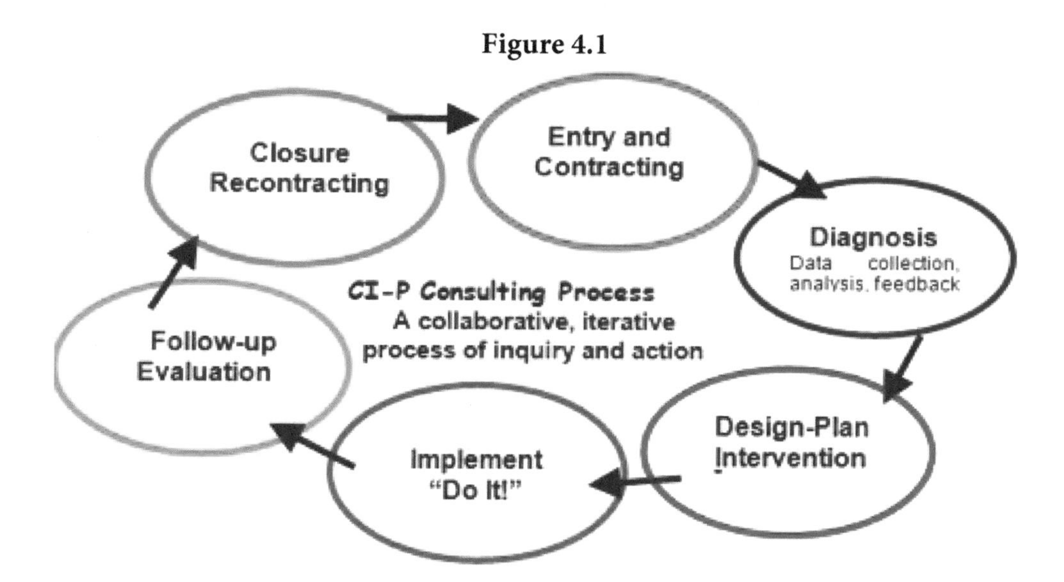

A face-to-face meeting was set up with the manager to determine what the problem was and how best to approach it. It was not uncommon for managers to want to use *BTC* to solve personnel problems dealing more with personalities and behaviors than process or system issues. This confusion often happened because of their lack of understanding of what a process was. These meetings were important instructional moments for managers.

The purpose of the initial entry and contracting meeting was to sort out whether the problem was a process/system issue amendable to Lean principles and methods or a personnel problem requiring a human resources (HR) solution. Once the CIP determined this was a problem that *BTC* could help with, the CIP and the "manager or sponsor" would complete a formal chartering document (see appendix C) to fully understand and document the perceived problem.

This included a statement of the perceived problem, current situation, expected outcome, outcome measures, and the various team roles and individuals who would be participating in the improvement event. As we worked with initial improvement teams, we learned that often the problem was not, in fact, what the manager thought it was. Keep in mind that most managers did not have a good understanding of process and systems and did not think of their problem(s) in these terms. One of the first points made in the initial meeting with a manager was to review the concept of a process with them and emphasize Deming's point that 94 percent of the problems in the work site are systems/process issues and *not* people issues.

Entry and Contracting: The entry and contracting stage were designed to establish relationships and potential problem/solution strategies between the sponsor and manager requesting a service and the CIP(s) who would be working with them. As *BTC* developed this, it became a standardized process in which a team of two CIPs interviewed a manager and/or sponsor to determine what was needed and how best to proceed. Participants in these meetings could include the sponsor responsible for removing barriers, the individual/manager who would affect the change(s), and, if different, the person requesting help. As *BTC* developed, the CIP team could also include individuals who were just out of a DOP training as observers learning from the interview process. In addition to the charter, often a formal contract was written specifying goals and objectives and responsibilities and commitment of the sponsor, manager, and the CIP team.

Diagnosis: Once there was agreement to move ahead, the CIP, in conjunction with various improvement team members, would request and review what data was available to further understand the nature of the problem. It was not unusual for the CIP team to find that relevant data was very limited if it existed at all. Often when sponsors or managers were asked how they knew there was a problem, they referred to a variety of amorphous issues such as customer complaints or a "feeling" that a process shouldn't take so long or there were "too many errors" (sometimes documented and sometimes not), backlogs that could be identified, or low morale, et cetera. When data was available, this was collected by the CIPs to serve as a baseline for improvements and to clarify problems. If appropriate and feasible, the CIP team would also go to the respective work site, *gemba*, to observe the situation and collect data when available.

Design and Plan the Intervention: This was a critical stage of the CIP consulting process and involved the CIP team that was planning the work for the improvement intervention. *BTC* developed a standard format to design all improvement interventions called "design notes" (see appendix B). This was a standardized format that was used to plan any event that CIPs were assigned to work on. The CIP team would set time aside, generally eight to ten hours, to plan an event, such as a value stream mapping or other improvement event. Design notes detailed the flow of how the improvement event was to unfold. They included activities that the team would participate in, questions to be asked, materials needed, and expected outcomes from various activities. The design notes were purposely designed to be so detailed that any CIP could pick them up and know what was to be done during an improvement event. This was done to assure not only that CIPs were following standard practice but also that if an assigned CIP could not be available for a session, another CIP could be called and step in to continue the work uninterrupted. The design notes proved to aid success in our improvement work because they provided confidence to the CIPs leading a session and because they followed a standard process that assured them they would achieve the intend outcome in the intended time frame. In addition, completing the design notes assured thoughtful and thorough planning by the CIP(s).

Standard Implementation: The implementation phase represented the actual improvement event that the CIP team was contracted to work on. Some espouse five days for an improvement effort, and we have done VSMs in as little as a half or one day, but we typically planned on three consecutive days. While sponsors were willing to give the CIP team three days, they sometimes resisted the idea of three consecutive days since that would mean they would have to shut down part of all their operations for that period, which often proved very difficult for them to do. CIPs struggled with this idea and eventually decided to meet customer demand by offering flexible options, including three full days over a period of three to four weeks. Note: this is one of the many teachable moments. What if the manager/supervisor knew that "this is the work" (i.e., this is not extra time; this is time to get it right and get it right the first time all of the time!)?

As we started out, CIPs would contract with the sponsor to work with the team for two consecutive full days starting at 8:00 a.m. and continuing to 5:00 p.m., including an hour for lunch and two fifteen-minute breaks, one in the morning and one in the afternoon. Day one was designed to work on the current state of the process, and day two the future state and implementation plan. It soon became clear that two days did not provide enough time to fully articulate the problem and deal with the complexity of the issues discovered. This was a big problem since one of the outcomes of the VSM event was to prioritize and document identified improvements. CIPs would then have to schedule an additional half day or more to complete the work. We soon realized we needed to contract for three full days.

Importantly, we recognized that most state employees had little knowledge of improvement and Lean concepts and thinking. Because Lean thinking and understanding were critical to building a Lean culture, the *BTC* facilitation strategy was designed not only to assist in process and other improvement but also to teach staff basic Lean concepts such as flow, process, waste, pull, cycle time, et cetera, while at the same time working with them to identify and make improvements.

Learn and Do: In addition to improving a process, we wanted to teach the improvement team a new way of thinking about problem-solving. In order to accomplish this, we designed the three-day improvement event to include what we called "learn and dos," which were designed to teach hands-on basic continuous improvement and Lean concepts. Adding the "learn and dos" into the improvement event also extended the time needed to complete the event, but we felt in the long run that as teams became familiar with Lean, The necessity of these 'learn and dos would diminish over time.

Figure 4.2 displays the overall standard intervention process used by CIPs for the implementation phase of the CIP consulting process. As *BTC* got started, many if not most of the problems CIPs worked on were process issues and therefore involved value stream mapping. For these, the goal of the improvement event was twofold: (1) to identify the problem by mapping out the current state of the process and (2) to teach the improvement team a new way of thinking about problem-solving.

Figure 4.2

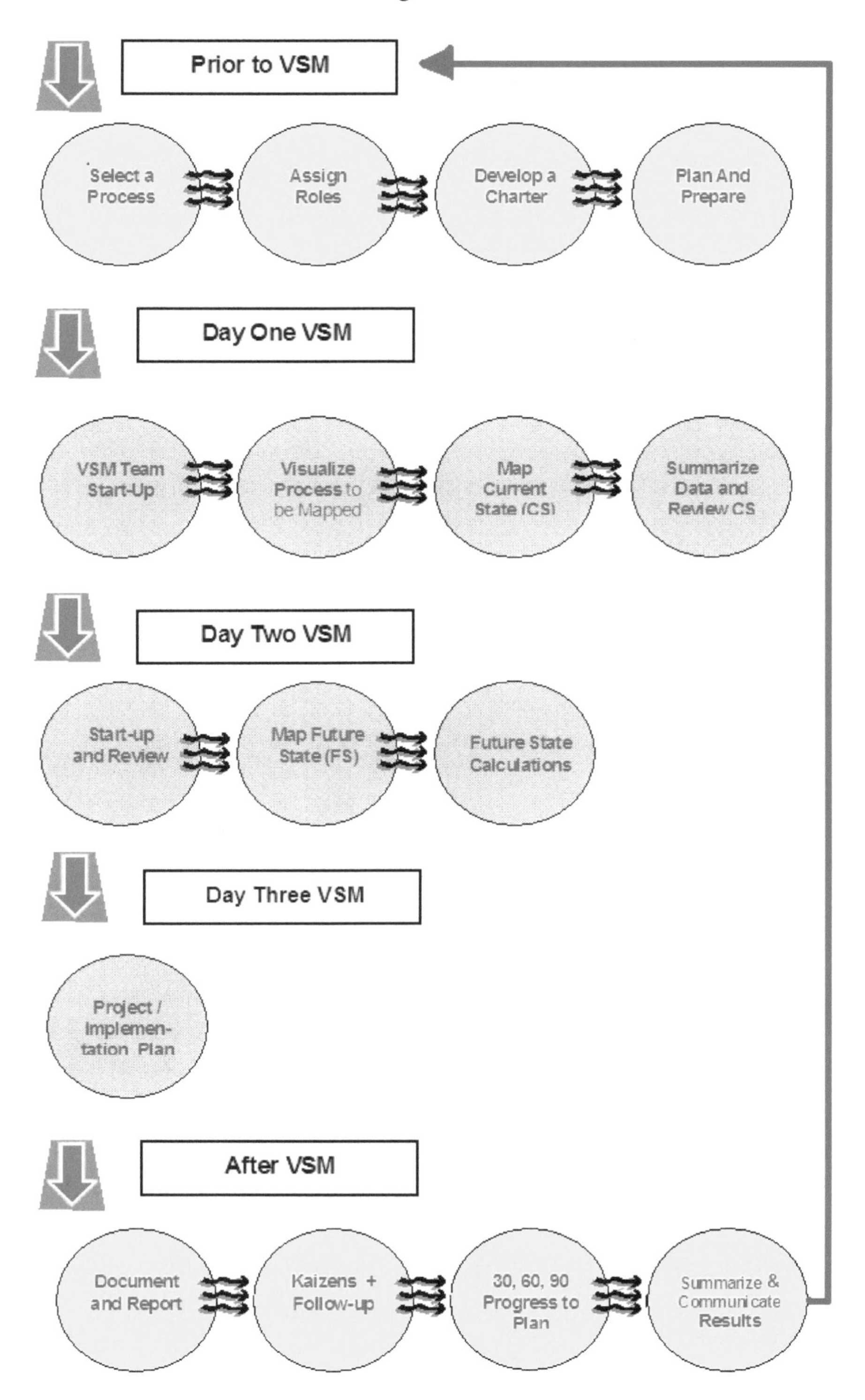
Prior to VSM
Select a Process
Assign Roles
Develop a Charter
Plan And Prepare
Day One VSM
VSM Team Start-Up
Visualize Process to be Mapped
Map Current State (CS)
Summarize Data and Review CS
Day Two VSM
Start-up and Review
Map Future State (FS)
Future State Calculations
Day Three VSM
Project / Implemen-tation Plan
After VSM
Document and Report
Kaizens + Follow-up
30, 60, 90 Progress to Plan
Summarize & Communicate Results

The CIP Team: A standard CIP team included a lead and co-lead and often included one or two CIP observers/interns. The CIP lead was one who had either completed the *BTC* certification process (to be discussed in the next chapter) or who had worked as co-lead for at least two or more improvement events and observed two events. The CIP lead was responsible for the entire deliverables for the improvement, including creating design notes, leading parts of or the entire three-day session, supervising/mentoring the co-lead and CIP observers, and providing documentation and follow-up work for the team. The co-lead generally was in a training capacity but was proficient enough in continuous improvement and Lean to be able to lead sections of the three-day event, depending on his/her experience and agreement with the Lead CIP, and these were assigned in advance of the session. Observers/interns were generally CIP trainees who were state employees who had just completed a DOP training and were sitting in to learn by observing the improvement event. They were required to actively observe and provide their observations and questions as feedback to the lead and co-lead at the end of each day. Otherwise, the observers played no active role in the event itself.

Cross-Training: The *BTC* CIP cadre came from various state departments. A CIP's primary role in an improvement event was to facilitate and to provide knowledge and direction for the sponsor, manager, and improvement team. While CIPs might also be expected to provide Lean leadership in their respective departments, they could also be assigned to lead improvement teams in other state departments. We found that CIPs leading teams in other departments had the advantage of being neutral with respect to the improvement teams' ideas and directions. It also broadened the perspective of the CIPs with respect to the types of improvement events they were able to manage. The downside was that they were not working exclusively in their assigned departments and, therefore, not available when they were working elsewhere. Generally, this did not prove to be a significant problem for *BTC*, and most CIPs assigned to events outside of their respective departments were able to do complete them. This cross-training also extends the skill and experience of the CIPs.

The Improvement Team: The members of each improvement team were assigned by the respective departmental sponsor and manager. Team size ranged from five to twenty-five members, although *BTC* preferred to work with teams no larger than twelve, which was a recommendation made to sponsors during entry and contracting. Team membership was drawn from those employees who were either working in the process or were very familiar with it. Generally, we saw team members with a wide range of experience, ranging from newly hired employees to twenty- to thirty-year veterans. In addition to the improvement sponsor and manager roles, there was an assigned data manager role, which was responsible for collecting data and working with data that was generated during the improvement event. Team members assigned to this role had to be willing to work with numbers and simple math. Individuals that had an investment in the outcome of the improvement team but could not attend the sessions were designated as caucus members, which meant that they could be called and could keep informed about the progress the team was making and/or answer questions that would come up that the improvement team could not answer. CIPs emphasized that their role was to facilitate the team and that the team itself would be the one to identify what the problem was and how best to improve it. Since much of government management is a "blame and shame" culture, the idea that their manager/sponsor was appealing to the team to actively identify problems and to help improve their work proved to be very rewarding and satisfying to them.

Developing a growing Lean knowledge in state staff was a key part of all *BTC* improvement efforts and was built into them. This was evident in their structure and content. While simply facilitating a team through a VSM would certainly take less time and effort, it would not begin to embed Lean thinking into the state culture (i.e., *as in teaching a person to fish…).*

Day 1—Developing the Current State: Day one began with a review of the completed charter to establish consensus on the problem to be worked on. It was often the case that the state improvement teams came into the session with an expectation that the CIPs were going to solve the problem for them, so it came as a surprise that they would be the ones to do this. Not unexpectedly, some expressed cynicism that anything would change. In part to allay such concerns, and as part of the implementation design, the CIP team developed and sent a pre-event pamphlet describing the VSM process to all participants. During the start of the day one session, a participant workbook was designed and handed out to each improvement team member. Table 1 displays a typical agenda for a three-day value stream mapping session. At the start of day one, the CIPs reviewed the content of the participant workbook (PW) with the improvement team and the schedule for each day. The PW was customized by the lead and co-lead for the respective intervention.

The focus on the first day of the intervention (day one) is to accurately map, "see," and measure the current process. This is accomplished by having the team develop a value stream map (VSM). The tendency on day one is to want to jump ahead and "fix" the process—to leap to solutions. CIPs on day one emphasized that before we could make improvements we needed to "see" and understand and get team consensus on the process as it currently is now: the current state. Participants were told that the goal for day one is to make their work "visible." This meant very little to them initially but, by the end of day one, proved to be very insightful and often a profound experience for them, since this was usually the first time they had seen and thought about their work as a process and how the dynamics of upstream and downstream work affected their work.

Table 1
Typical VSM Agenda

Intervention Name:

Morning	Afternoon
Day One: ________	12:00 • *Lunch* (on your own)
8:15 • Start-up & Agenda • Charter • Team Roles 9:00 • Improvement Project Mission 9:40 • Systems & Process Thinking 10:30 • *Break* 10:45 • Process Matrix	12:30 • Flow Activity 1:15 • Begin Visualizing Current State 2:15 • *Break* 2:30 • Complete Mapping Current State 4:15 • Summary & Next Steps 4:30 • Adjourn
Day Two: ________	12:00 • *Lunch* (on your own)
8:15 • Start-up 8:30 • COMPLETE CS TIMES 10:00 • *Break* 10:15 • Waste/Lean Concepts 11:00 • Analysis/Prepare for FS Mapping	12:30 • Begin Future Process Mapping 2:15 • *Break* 2:30 • Continue Future Process Mapping 4:15 • Wrap-up/Feedback & Adjourn 4:30 • Adjourn
Day Three: ________	12:00 • *Lunch* (on your own)
8:00 • Start-up 8:30 • COMPLETE FS STEPS & TIMES 9:30 • Review & Analyze CS, FS, & Times Calc. 9:55 • Improvement Imp. Plan Concepts 10:15 • *Break* 10:30 • Identify/Brainstorm Change Activities 11:15 • Begin Prioritizing Changes	12:30 • Begin Creating Improvement Imp. Plan 2:15 • *Break* 2:30 • Finish Improvement Imp. Plan 4:00 • Follow-up/Next Steps 4:15 • Wrap-up/Feedback & Adjourn 4:30 • Adjourn

When the improvement team saw the completed value stream map, it was often a transformative experience for them. One goal for the session was to change the way the improvement team viewed their work, and this was achieved almost 100 percent of the time. It was not unusual to hear team members say something like, "No wonder I can't get my work done." Or "All this time I thought I was the problem." Or "This finally shows what I've been trying to say all along." Or "Wow, it is so complicated!"

An additional objective of day one is to teach some basic Lean and continuous improvement concepts to employees who rarely thought in these terms. These concepts were then immediately applied to their particular problem or process they were working on in day one. A complete map like the one in Figure 4.3 is generally completed on day one of the intervention.

Figure 4.3
A Typical Current State Map

The team collected relevant measures for the process such as elapsed time and value-added and total lead time. The VSM enables the team to immediately begin to identify where the problems are in their process and to start thinking about improvement ideas. Although the purpose of day one was not to identify and document improvements, it was impossible for the flaws in the process not to become apparent and for improvement ideas to occur to team members. The CIPs explained that team participants could note improvement ideas on Post-it notes, which they could post throughout the session on a flip chart to be reviewed and used in day two. Day one always proved to be hard work for both the improvement team and the CIP team. By the end of the day, team members were tired but satisfied that they had learned something of value and were excited about the possibilities for improving their work. This was almost always a new experience for them and generated a lot of discussion and excitement about their work. It also got the team working and talking together. Some described this as "the soft side of Lean" (i.e., the improved communication and understanding among team members), a phenomena Jody Hoffer Gittell calls "relational coordination" (RC), as opposed to the technical "hard" concepts of Lean (i.e., the current, future state maps and improved plans, 5S, et cetera). RC is defined as coordinating work through high-quality communication supported by relationships of shared goals, shared knowledge, and mutual respect. The diagram 4.3 below depicts these relationships.

Diagram 4.3: The dynamics of improvement practices

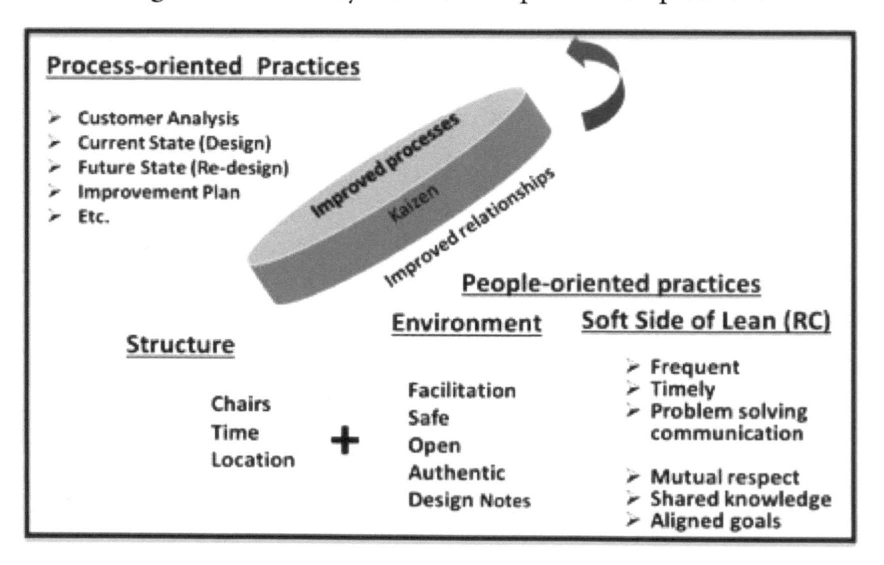

Day 2—Developing the Future State: As is previously mentioned, each day started with a training tutorial. The goals for day two included analyzing the current state, introducing additional Lean concepts and techniques, identifying the eight wastes, other vital and formation in regards to "the language of process improvement" as well as techniques for creating a future state map. The current state (CS) map was always front and center in the session. These maps were developed on brown "butcher" paper rolled out and hung on a wall with worksheets and Post-it notes to capture process steps and the data about them. The future state map was developed on a butcher paper hung above the current state map for easy reference.

Day two was almost always easier on the teams because after the effort put into creating the current state map and the conceptual dissonance it provided for the team (i.e., seeing their work differently for the first time), by the time the team got to day two, they were ready and eager to tackle the improvement effort. Day two generally began by reviewing day one's work and tying up any loose ends. We then jumped into a brief "learn and do" activity on the eight wastes. This was followed by brainstorming what the future state would look like and what changes needed to be made to create it. Brainstorming often occurred by breaking the whole improvement team down into small groups and letting them work uninterrupted for a brief period before bringing them back together to summarize their findings. Improvement ideas from day one was reviewed, and ideas from the brainstorming sessions were captured along with specific improvement actions and data estimates of how these improvements would impact lead time, work time, and other value metrics. These were completed as the team developed the future state map. This mapping often was very creative, and the team readily worked with the Lean concepts learned in day one to generate the future state map, a final mapping of process improvement steps/ideas and estimated measures the new process could be expected to achieve if all the improvement ideas were implemented.

Day 3—Developing the Improvement Action Plan: The tutorial focus of day three was to give the team "license" to imagine a better process, a process that would eliminate the eight wastes. For some CIPs, it was also the case that they had to dissuade improvement team members skillfully and supportively and/or tactfully from leaping to solutions that depended on information technology. The CIPs recognized that the process improvement team had made their work flow visible for the first time.. The goal of day three was to develop a completed improvement action plan that included identifying what changes were to be implemented, prioritizing them, establishing a date for completion, and identifying who was responsible for seeing that the change happened. Improvement changes often needed to be broken down into specific tasks, which were prioritized and assigned to specific team members who were interested in seeing that the specific tasks were completed.

Overall responsibility for completing the implementation plan was assigned to the sponsor/VS manager, with the VS manager having the day-to-day responsibility for seeing the improvement work got done. This required the VS manager to free up time for the improvement team members to meet and work on their respective tasks, which often provoked some resistance and challenges for from managers regarding "more work" (see sidebar). This was an important and critical responsibility for the manager. The CIP team encouraged them to work on tasks in "chunks" of time (a half day, full day, or more) rather than the typical state government strategy of meeting once a week for an hour for months on end. The idea behind meeting for a half day or full day to report on and do the improvement tasks was that the team could do focused work and complete the improvement in a timely way, as well as identify problems/barriers encountered and seek solutions for them. The rationale given here was that if the improvement was causing a pain for the customer or the improvement team, which was costing them time, money, or other resources, then fixing it quickly made sense. This was similar to Toyota's stopping the line to fix something immediately. Whenever items could be fixed immediately, we encouraged the team to fix them. It was not uncommon, for example, that once the improvement team saw a map of their process, they began to identify things that were problematical and sometimes would come back to the day two session with the improvement already in place. CIPs were responsible for facilitating the ongoing work with these teams as necessary and working with the sponsor/VS manager to set a follow-up schedule with the whole improvement team. At the end of day three, a feedback questionnaire was handed out to the team to gather data on their experiences over the three-day event. These were generally very positive, providing useful feedback for *BTC* to further improve its work.

Follow-up and Evaluation: Once the improvement action plan (IAP) was complete, CIPs would continue to work with the improvement team, sharing his/her Lean expertise, to assist them in completing identified improvement tasks. The work accomplished by the VSM team was documented, and a report, including the CS and FS maps and the implementation plan, presented to the sponsor and manager. The IAP developed was addressed, using project management tools and techniques. The team was encouraged to minimally report and measure progress on the plan on at least thirty-, sixty-, and ninety-day intervals and at least monthly intervals thereafter with all results documented and reported.

Often some identified improvements were significant pieces of work, related processes, et cetera, requiring separate, distinct improvement efforts (kaizen or rapid improvement events) and were documented to be addressed. These new teams could be made up of participants in the VSM work but also could recruit other staff who either worked in the process or had a significant interest in wanting to see the process improved. The CIP lead and co-lead would organize and facilitate these follow-up sessions.

The report, including the improvement action plan, was presented to the sponsor, usually with the entire improvement team present. This was an opportunity for the sponsor to see the current and future state maps and to hear about the opportunities available for improvement, barriers that might require the sponsor's intervention, and estimated savings in time, manpower, error reduction in the process, potential impact on upstream and downstream processes, and improvements that might require additional expenditures. The presence of the entire team at this meeting provided an opportunity for the improvement team to explain the team reasoning for recommended changes and the benefits these changes would have for the process and end user (the customer). This meeting was also a great opportunity for the entire team along with the sponsor and VS manager to align their work with the overall mission of the organization in meeting respective customer needs.

Closure and Re-contracting. CIPs encouraged improvement teams to complete their work with three to six months, depending upon the complexity of the work to be done. The event was considered closed when either all the identified improvements on the improvement action plan were completed or that additional improvement work was no longer possible. This could be the case if completed improvements eliminated problems that had been identified to be worked on but were no longer a problem or that the scope of changes required went beyond the boundaries of the particular department in question. Sometimes changes were stalled because potential improvements required additional funding that was not immediately available.

Re-contracting was done when one improvement project was completed, and the sponsor/VS manager wanted to work on a new improvement project/process. Re-contracting could involve the same CIP and improvement team or new teams with different CIPs and participants. In any case, the standard consulting process was followed as described above.

You cannot hear what you do not understand.
—W. Edwards Deming

CHAPTER 5: STANDARD MATERIALS

This chapter describes the standardized materials that *BTC* developed to assist CIPs in their improvement practice. A major goal of *BTC* was to transform how state employees viewed how "work works" by developing a Lean mindset. As noted, before, Lean principles and methods were basically unknown to state workers and managers at all levels. Those who enrolled to become a CIP and the Lean/CIP trainers and facilitators also initially had little to no background in Lean. Once practitioners completed the DOP, it was clear that they needed additional materials to support their improvement practice. *BTC* developed standard materials, forms, and workbooks that incorporated Lean methods and approaches as guides for CIP practitioners to support and sustain the standard processes and practices that were taught in the DOP.

As we learned what worked and what did not for government employees, we continuously improved these materials to more effectively meet the needs of the teams the CIPs were working with (i.e., we applied Lean/CI to our *BTC* processes as well). Over time these became highly effective tools that CIPs could rely upon to assure that they were able to achieve success with improvement teams. One of the primary tasks CIPs were asked to perform was to facilitate process improvement teams. Value stream mapping generally proved to be one of the first improvement activities that CIPS were involved with since so many of *BTC's* requests for services were broken or inefficient processes. Therefore, we worked on developing a standard set of VSM materials for CIPs to use with improvement teams. These are described below and included a standard kit of materials that contain all mapping materials, standard pre-improvement workbooks and participant workbooks, standard handouts, and forms in printed and electronic format.

Standard VSM materials: The improvement role for employees who became CIPs included not only their regular assigned work within their respective departments but also outside their departments as well. In addition to chartering and contracting, CIPS worked with a sponsor or VSM manager to arrange for space for the improvement event and to coordinate schedules with the improvement team, which could range from one to three days consecutively or across several weeks. When CIPs worked with improvement teams, they were responsible for all materials needed for an improvement event, including those necessary to successfully create a value stream map. As we became more experienced, to avoid problems of omissions and forgetfulness, we developed a standard VSM kit, which contained all the materials CIPs would need to successfully complete a VSM or other improvement event. These materials were stored in a standardized carrying box, with several of these kits made up, ready for use, and stored in a central location. A picture of one of these kits and a CIP workbook is displayed above. CIPs using the kit were responsible for picking it up, returning it, and assuring the contents were complete and restocked. The kit contents are listed in appendix F. *BTC* used brown "butcher" or mailing paper thirty inches wide and often ten to twenty feet long to construct value stream maps with the improvement teams. The use of 'smart sheets' has become another useful media to render VSM maps. The current state (CS) and future state (FS) maps were constructed on two separate sheets, with the future state displayed over the current state, so the entire current and future state could be viewed simultaneously as the FS was being constructed. These maps could be rolled up and stored for future use or moved to other locations if necessary. The butcher paper allowed CIPs to write on it, draw lines such as swim lanes, information technology connections, or other notations such as needed kaizen bursts. The improvement teams were encouraged to take these maps back to their work site and post them so other staff could see the work that was done and provide additional input to the team. Electronic versions of these maps and improvement action plan were also created in order to maximize sharing and assure a permanent record.

Separate sheets were printed to identify each process step and collect its data. These were standardized as to color, size, and content—salmon for current state and green for future state. The number of data sheets used was dependent on the complexity or granularity (i.e., level of detail) of the process. The process bookends—the beginning step and ending step—and granularity were generally determined in advance with the sponsor and manager and would be confirmed with the team before the mapping began.

> Most state employees had no idea of process improvement and did not have any idea of the concept of process and workflow itself. While all state employees were involved in meetings to solve problems, these meetings were generally not process oriented and met sporadically weekly or monthly—for an hour or so—over several months, until the problem was solved or forgotten. Since no one saw problems from a system/processes perspective, they rarely worked together as an intact process improvement team. For many, a process improvement session was a first-time experience, particularly working with teammates in taking a dedicated period to fully understand and identify root-cause issues. Additionally, most understood there was waste in the workplace but did not have a formal concept of waste or the tools to identify it.

Design Notes: Design notes (DN) were customized by CIPs for every improvement encounter, including training and improvement events. The purpose of the design notes was threefold: first, to provide a standard format for presenting information to a group; second to ensure that the presentation is well planned in advance of the actual session; and third, to provide a constant reference point during the sessions for CIPs. In the latter case, DNs allowed for CIPs to step in to an improvement event if the primary CIP was not available. Design notes were developed in advance for each day of a VSM event by the CIP lead and co-lead. An agenda outline for a typical current state day one design note for a value stream mapping session is shown below in Table 5.1, with a typical example displayed in appendix C. While the detailed content of DNs for each event will vary for each improvement session, the basic structure of the DN did not vary and followed the structure in Table 5.1.

The time durations were organized around modules, and each module was designed to flow into the next one. Necessary concepts were taught, generally using a "learn and do" approach, and these concepts were used to build upon in the next module with the overall goal of applying newly acquired concepts to the improvement work. Note that time was scheduled before the session, usually one hour, for the CIPs to set the room and review activities for the day—done by reviewing the design notes by the CIP team.

Since this approach to process improvement was a new experience for improvement team members, the first part of the day one was spent introducing team members, reviewing the charter and the problem statement, and introducing basic Lean/CI principles and methods. (Note: PW below refers to the participant workbook.)

Table 5.1
CI Practitioner's Detailed Agenda:
Day One of Three-Day VSM

7:00–8:00 CIP Set-up and Prep for VSM

- Orient yourself
- Assemble materials (VSM supplies/materials kit)
- Prepare room
- Set up computer
- Practitioner team "huddle"

8:00–8:30 Start-Up in VSM Teams

- Introduce practitioner team
- Sponsor/manager welcome
- Participant introductions
- Logistics and overview
- One-page overview of three days (PW p. 20)
- Roles and responsibilities (PW p. 5–6)

8:30–8:45 Team Charter

- VSM manager reviews charter with Ps (PW p. 8–11)
- Identify data manager if have not already

8:45–9:15 Visualize Process to Be Mapped

- Worksheet: Visualize process to be mapped (PW p. 23)
- Individual brainstorm
- Round-robin posting
- Sort and group
- Transition process mindset

9:15–10:00 Lean Concepts

- Elicit from team: What is Lean?
- Review principles (PW pp. 18–19)
- Flow activity or input
  (See separate design notes for flow activity)

10:00–10:15 Worksheet VS and NVA

- Worksheet: Value versus Nonvalue added (PW p. 24)
- Option: individual, pairs, trios
- Debrief worksheet and provide teaching points

10:15–10:30 Break

- Meet with CI practitioner team

10:30–12:00 Current State Mapping and Data Sheets

- Worksheet: Current state mapping (PW p. 26)
- What is the step just before this bookend?
- Document three decisions
- Data sheet definitions (PW p. 29)

12:00–12:30 Lunch

- Meet with CI practitioner team
- FC questions if haven't already

12:30–2:15 Current State Map, Continued

2:15–2:30 Break

- Meet with CI practitioner team
- Assess where team is and make adjustments as needed

2:30–3:30 Current State Map, Continued

- Finish mapping

3:30–4:00 Current State Calculations

- Worksheet: Calculating current state metrics (PW p. 31)
    - Review current state data
- Review practical tips

4:00-4:30 Checkout and Assignment

- Give assignments
- Round-robin checkout

Prework Materials: Often improvement team members were not clear as to why they were even coming to an improvement event. Many participants thought that the CIP team was there to tell them how to improve their work! Initially, we spent considerable time during the first day explaining what Lean/CI was about and how CIPs intended to work with them. This was facilitated by using a PowerPoint presentation; however, we were not satisfied with this approach because the PowerPoint presentation was not engaging and took considerable time. As a result, we eliminated the PowerPoint altogether and developed a preworkshop handout, which provided a brief overview of Bend the Curve and what the team could expect to happen during an improvement session and briefly answered the questions "What is Lean?" and "What is the improvement process?" The preworkshop handout included a copy of the charter of the work to be accomplished and roles and responsibilities of team members involved in the improvement work. This preworkshop handout was sent to the sponsor for distribution to the team members to emphasize that this was a management-initiated effort and supported by the sponsor.

Participant Workbook: As part of standardizing *BTC* process improvement work, we developed a participant workbook (PW) to be given to every member of the improvement team on the first day of the improvement event. The PW served two purposes: first, to provide a guide and relevant materials for the session as well as basic Lean/CI concepts and second, to provide an ongoing reference for the improvement team members when they returned to their respective work site. The PW followed a standard format as displayed in Table 2 but was customized for the event or problem that a given team was working on. The PW was developed as the CIPs were developing their design notes for the event so that page numbers in the PW were keyed off the design notes used by the CIPs team.

The PW was handed out at the beginning of an improvement event and was reviewed at the start of the event and referenced throughout the event session. The PW contains schedules for the events, agendas, the charter, definition of key terms, activity worksheets for the "learn and dos," and other forms that were used during the improvement session. For example, Table 3 displays an overview of a typical agenda for a three-day VSM. Listed are the various modules used and the amount of time estimated for each module. Times, of course, could be flexed—longer or shorter—if the necessity arose, depending on the size of the team and their knowledge of the process. Teams that successfully improved their work process often used this approach to improve additional work processes. The teams that had been through one or more VSM event and were familiar with Lean/CI principles and methods did not need to go through all the details portrayed here and could jump right into working on their process.

The PW displayed the agenda for the three days that we typically used to work with teams who were new to process improvement work. Day one was designed to familiarize the team members to the overall VSM process, the process problem they would be working on, group dynamics, and basic Lean concepts of process and workflow and developing a current state map. With the help of the standardized design notes and PW, the CIPs were generally able to successfully complete this agenda and develop a current state map in the time allotted, day one. On occasion, if a process proved to be more complex or the bookends (i.e., start and end of the process) were not set properly and needed to be adjusted, the current state mapping session might spill over into day two, and the scheduled would need to be adjusted accordingly. Day two was focused on reviewing the current state map, learning about waste, and developing the future state map. Day three was focused on developing the improvement action plan and the follow-up strategy, which would include meeting updates and kaizen events.

Making Work Visible: Each day ended with a brief evaluation of the session and a plan for next steps. Since government employees had never experienced this type of improvement work, many felt "stunned" and fascinated at realizing how intricate and complex their work was and how much waste there was in their work and why there were problems in it. CIPs emphasized the notion of "making their work visible" at the beginning of a session. Few participants at the time knew what this meant, but by the end of the day, all understood what it meant and how important it was for them to understand how their "work worked." Once team members understood how a tool like a VSM could be used, they began immediately to see opportunities for improvement and also understand why they were often so frustrated by their inability to get their work done without error or delays. Concepts of workflow and waste were also well understood by the end of the improvement event.

Table 2 Participant Workbook—Table of Contents

Table 2 Participant Workbook—Table of Contents (Continued)

Table 3

Intervention Name:	
Day One: __________	**12:00** · ***Lunch*** (on your own)
8:15 · Start-Up and Agenda · Charter · Team Roles **9:00** · Improvement Project Mission **9:40** · Systems and Process Thinking **10:30** · *Break* **10:45** · Process Matrix	**12:30** · Flow Activity **1:15** · Begin Visualizing Current State **2:15** · *Break* **2:30** · Complete Mapping Current State **4:15** · Summary and Next Steps **4:30** · Adjourn
Day Two: __________	**12:00** · ***Lunch*** (on your own)
8:15 · Start-Up **8:30 · Complete CS Times** **10:00** · *Break* **10:15** · Waste/Lean Concepts **11:00** · Analysis/Prepare for FS Mapping	**12:30** · Begin Future Process Mapping **2:15** · *Break* **2:30** · Continue Future Process Mapping **4:15** · Wrap-up/Feedback and Adjourn **4:30** · Adjourn
Day Three: __________	**12:00** · ***Lunch*** (on your own)
8:00 · Start-Up **8:30 · Complete FS Steps and Times** **9:30** · Review and Analyze CS, FS, and Times Calculations **9:55** · Improvement Implementation Plan Concepts **10:15** · *Break* **10:30** · Identify/Brainstorm Change Activities **11:15** · Begin Prioritizing Changes	**12:30** · Begin Creating Improvement Implementation Plan **2:15** · *Break* **2:30** · Finish Improvement Implementation Plan **4:00** · Follow-Up/Next Steps **4:15** · Wrap-Up/Feedback and Adjourn **4:30** · Adjourn

Standard Technology: Standard technology refers to equipment such as computers; projectors; printers, including color, large capacity front and back, and poster printers; Microsoft (MS) Office products, such as PowerPoint (PPT), Excel, and Visio; web pages; posters; and simulations that *BTC* used in its improvement events or training sessions. These items were either routinely used in sessions or were readily available to be used should the need arise. Some of these items such as web pages were available twenty-four seven for the convenience of CIPs and improvement team members.

Hardware and Software: In training and improvement events, we found it useful to have available a laptop and projector and a screen if a clear wall was not available. The laptop was a standard issue government computer that featured the MS Office suite containing MS Word, PowerPoint, and Excel. In the development of practitioner (DOP) training sessions, we used the laptop and projector mainly for PowerPoint slides that followed the training script for the day. The PowerPoint slides contained daily/weekly agendas, definitions, illustrations of key concepts and principles, and so on. Copies of the PPT slides were made available to the participants.

A laptop and projector were also available and used in the improvement events for PPT presentations and for displaying Excel spreadsheets. The latter was used for developing improvement plans or for summarizing data collected during VSM sessions. As mentioned earlier, in the *BTC* initial rollout, CIPs used a standard PPT slide deck to illustrate key Lean/CI concepts and principles. This supported CIPs' understanding and ability to use these concepts in kaizen events. Keep in mind that even though CIPs had been through an initial forty-hour (or longer) training, they still were new to these ideas; hence the PPT slides kept them on track and assured that these ideas were presented to the improvement team correctly.

Over time we eventually eliminated PPT slides entirely from improvement events, replacing them with "learn and do" activities and/or simulations to illustrate these concepts. Examples are discussed below. We found this approach was an improvement over the slides since it involved active "hands-on" learning by the improvement team members and hence held their interest and helped illustrate basic concepts more concretely.

Learn and Do: *BTC* developed "learn and do" activities for CIPs to use with improvement teams to illustrate basic Lean/CI concepts. One example is illustrated in Table 4. Most government workers were not familiar with the idea that all work is a process. They rarely saw their work from a process or system perspective, and while they often nodded "yes" when ask if they knew about process improvement, we found that generally most of their ideas were rudimentary at best. Hence, in a process improvement event, it was important to assure that the improvement team members had a solid grounding in the concepts of process and system thinking.

Rather than lecturing and using PPT, *BTC* developed a simple interactive exercise called "Walking the Dog" to help them understand system and process thinking—see the worksheet below. Team members are assigned to small groups and asked to complete this process activity for one of the four or five listed simple processes that they perform daily such as Walking the Dog, making coffee, getting to work on time, et cetera. The worksheet graphic was printed off in poster size and taped to the wall for each small group so that they could all "cluster" around and complete it. They were given ten to fifteen minutes to work among themselves and then present their work and decisions to the whole team. For example, for the group selecting Walking the Dog, the decisions about who is the client and what the product and outcome are can be interesting (and fun). The lead CIP facilitates the session, clarifying ideas and asking additional questions to assure that the group understands and can describe a process. The team's learning is then applied to the work process that they are about to improve. Similar types of learn and dos and simulations to illustrate Lean/CI methods and principles were used in the DOPs and the improvement events and will be illustrated in a companion volume.

Table 4
Learn and Do for System and Process Thinking

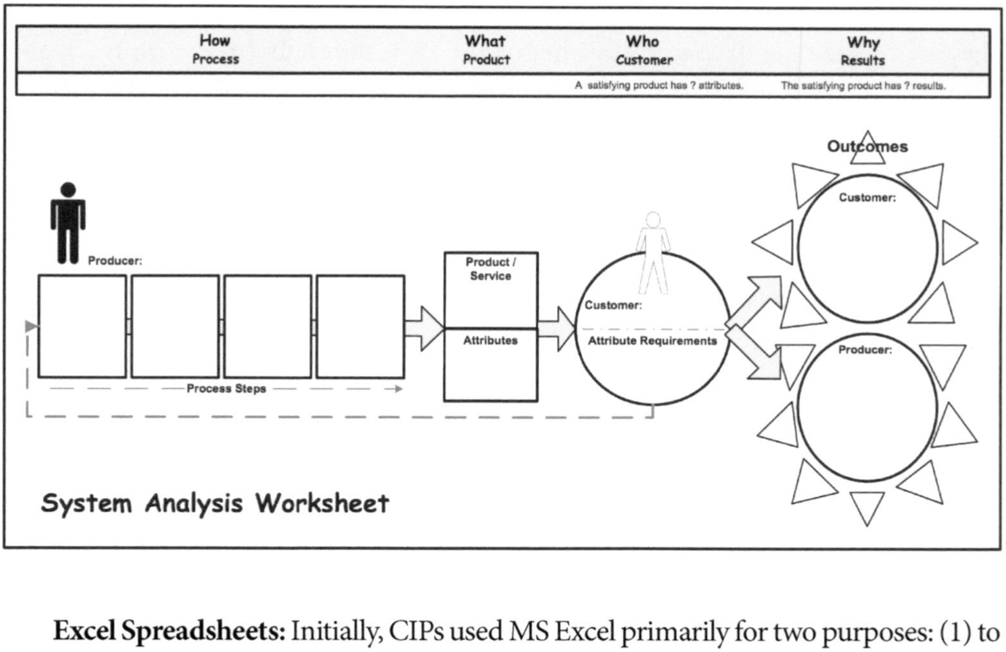

How
Process
What
Product
Who
Customer
Why
Results
A satisfying product has ? attributes.
The satisfying product has ? results.
Outcomes
Customer:
Producer:
Product / Service
Attributes
Customer:
Attribute Requirements
Producer:
Process Steps
System Analysis Worksheet

Excel Spreadsheets: Initially, CIPs used MS Excel primarily for two purposes: (1) to create real-time improvement plans with the improvement team and (2) to calculate the amount of time and money saved when the improvements tasks were fully implemented. Initially, the third day of a VSM improvement event was used to take all the improvement ideas generated by the team to create an improvement plan. Using a computer and projector, the CIPs would work with the team to complete the improvement plan. While this was an efficient way to create an improvement plan, it turned out to be problematic for several reasons. First, some CIPs were not proficient in using Excel, hence slowing the plan development process down considerably. Second, there were occasional technical problems that would derail the process. Third, team members found the process tedious and thus were not fully engaged. Fourth, the CIPs often had to do additional editing after the session was over, or we had to bring the team back if there were technical delays to complete the work. In keeping with the "learn and do" approach, *BTC* switched from using the laptop and projector in the session to a more dynamic and hands-on approach to create the improvement plan. This involved each team member brainstorming improvement ideas using Post-its and looping and grouping them on a blank poster sheet—and from that developing the action plan. This allowed the entire improvement team to be more actively engaged in its creation and complete the plan quickly. Staff responsible for specific tasks would know immediately and could begin to work on them as soon as possible.

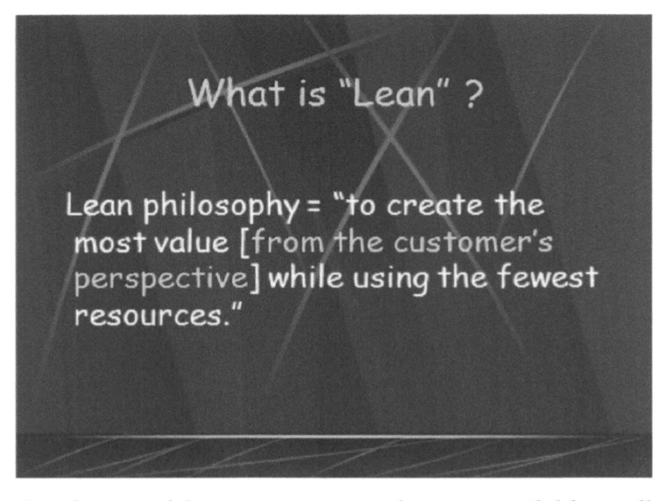

The one downside of this approach was that the CIPs were charged with keying the material on the poster into an Excel sheet after the session was completed so that a hard copy of the improvement plan was available to all the team members, as well as others who were involved or might be interested.

Posters: *BTC* developed a series of two-foot-by-three-foot posters that were laminated and used as needed at continuous improvement events. These posters displayed team norms and definitions of Lean, listed causes of waste, and depicted process flows and other relevant materials referred to when CIPs worked with improvement teams. These posters became particularly useful when we no longer relied exclusively on PPT presentations. The posters were hung on the walls in the room where an improvement event was taking place to be visible to the improvement team throughout the session. A typical poster is displayed above.

Standard Cost: One of the key goals for *BTC* was to convince management that the Lean methods and principles work by documenting savings and eliminating waste. *BTC* realized that it needed to capture gains and improvements and share them with the improvement teams and management. As *BTC* was rolled out, an Excel spreadsheet, the "metrics calculator," was developed and used to compare costs saved between current state and proposed future state gains. A key *BTC* member used MDOL in-house personnel statistics to develop an estimate of the average, but fully burdened, amount of money it cost to employ a staff person for one minute. We could therefore translate minutes saved into actual dollars saved. This made it possible to also collect savings totals across multiple improvement events. The metrics calculator was available to all CIPS involved in working with improvement teams.

Quantifying the Cost of Labor: Since one of the biggest costs in government is labor, we needed to find a way to calculate this cost. This was derived as the total personal services and personal benefits costs divided by the total work time. The total work time is defined as minutes in regular work status less adjustments for breaks, lunch, any time paid but not working—time available for hands-on work. In manufacturing it is known as the "fully burdened cost" of labor. At the time, we calculated this cost to be fifty-eight cents a minute for an average employee. We considered this be the standard cost for one minute of time for an average state of Maine employee during the time period *BTC* was in operation.

When value stream maps were developed, the fifty-eight cents were then used to calculate how much it cost in terms of time to perform a process step, or task, in a value stream. This number was then multiplied by "staff time," the number of people involved in performing the task, and the number of minutes to do that task to get a total cost for that step. For current state statistics, this number included all value-added and nonvalue-added time. These times (costs) were then aggregated across the current state, giving a total cost to produce one product or service going through the current state process. This number was then multiplied by the number of products or services provided in one year to achieve a total annual cost for the value stream with respect employee time. Additional costs identified, such as paper, computer time, copying, stamps, et cetera were documented for the process and were added as well.

A similar process was used in calculating cost for the future state; however, in this case the staff time costs were estimates of what the improvement team judged could be achieved when the process improvement ideas were implemented and all nonvalue-added costs (waste) eliminated. As with the current state process, these were aggregated for a year to estimate potential total annual savings once the improvements were completed.

These numbers for both the current and future state were then entered into the Excel spreadsheet (i.e., the metrics calculator) to produce a series of statistics and charts to compare overall annual savings for the process. An example of the output from the metrics calculator is displayed in Tables 6 and 7 and Figure 5.1.

*Developed by John Rioux

Table 6

Group Name			HETL Environmental Lab	
Cycles Per Year			220	
Other Savings, If Any			$0	
	Current	Future	Change	Yearly Savings
Steps (Number)	16	14	2	440
Lead Time *	281	28	252	55,495
Customer Non-Value Added Time *	266	20	246	54,138
Staff Time *	36	23	13	2,959
Cycle (Unit) Cost	$1,263	$795	$468	$102,973
Total Cost	$277,913	$174,940	$102,973	

Table 6 displays data from an improvement session with the Health and Environmental Testing Lab in which current and future state value stream maps were created. The summary data indicates the improvements in reducing the number steps, downtime, nonvalue-added time, staff time, and overall unit cost and total cost. Table 7 provides a more detailed breakdown of this data from the metric calculator. Figure 8 is a graphical display of the savings from this improvement event. These and other charts were reported to the improvement team and sponsor for them to assess the potential overall improvements and savings available to them if the improvement plan developed by the team is completed.

Standard Space—The Lean Lab: Government operations, such as a DOT licensing office, are often difficult to shut down during business hours since public expectations are that they are open when needed. In addition, office space was often not suitable for an improvement team to work in or stop activities, and usually space and meeting rooms were at a premium and often overbooked.

Initially, CIPs switched state office schedules to arrange meeting space for the time necessary to complete an improvement event, which generally ran from one to four days, with the average being three days. This meant that the actual improvement session would have to stop at the end of day one, and all materials would have to be removed and once again set up on another day, often days later.

This interruption impeded the continuity of the improvement process and proved to be time consuming with setup and reviewing where the team had left off.

Metrics Template For: HETL Environmental Lab			
Current State		**Future State**	
Steps =	**16**	**Steps =**	**14**
Lead Time (all C-T) =	**16,835**	**Lead Time (all C-T) =**	**1,700**
Value Added Time (V-A) =	**874**	**Value Added Time (V-A) =**	**504**
Non-Value Added (NV-A) =	**15961**	**Non-Value Added (NV-A) =**	**1196**
Time Associated With Inventory =	**2,373,360**	**Time Associated With Inventory =**	**114,435**
Steps in process that requires more focus on inventory		Steps in process that requires more focus on inventory	
Change Over Time (C-O-T) =	**0**	**Change Over Time (C-O-T) =**	**0**
Steps in process that requires more focus on amount COT		Steps in process that requires more focus on amount COT	
Up Time (U-T) =		**Up Time (U-T) =**	
Steps in Process that have a low Up-Time, requiring more focus	**10, 12, 13, 15**	Steps in Process that have a low Up-Time, requiring more focus	
First Pass Yield (FPY) =		**First Pass Yield (FPY) =**	
Steps in the process that have low First-Pass yield, requiring more attention.	**8, 12,**	Steps in the process that have low First-Pass yield, requiring more attention.	
Staff Time =	**2,178**	**Staff Time =**	**1,371**
Unit Cost =	**$1,263**	**Unit Cost =**	**$795**
Per Minute Staff Cost = $	0.58	**Total Savings Current vs. Future =**	**$468**
		Number of Units Per Year*	**220**
		Yearly Savings =	**$102,973**
		Other Savings =	$ -
* **Assume Value Stream represents 1 day's throughput.**		**Total Savings =**	**$102,973**

Table 7

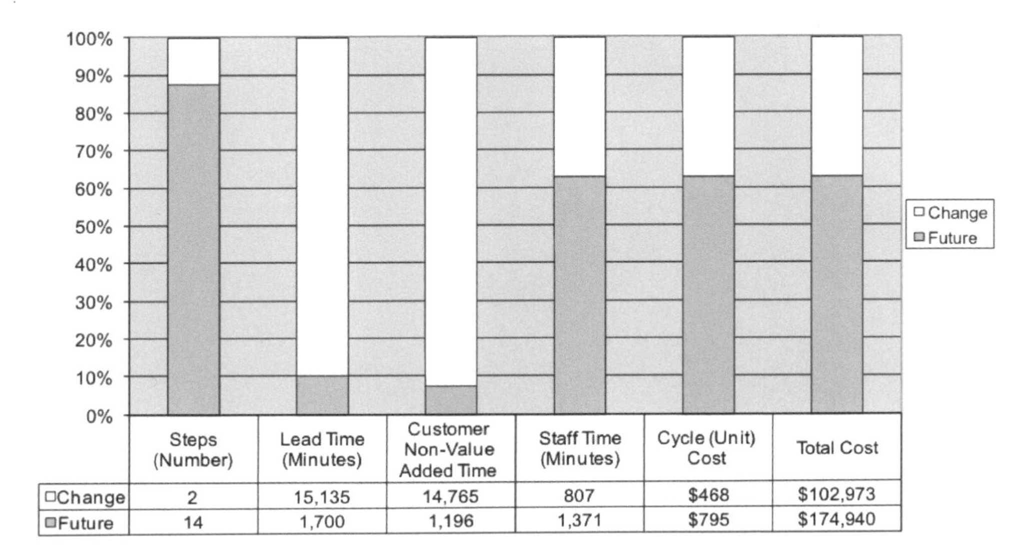

	Steps (Number)	Lead Time (Minutes)	Customer Non-Value Added Time	Staff Time (Minutes)	Cycle (Unit) Cost	Total Cost
Change	2	15,135	14,765	807	$468	$102,973
Future	14	1,700	1,196	1,371	$795	$174,940

Figure 8

The DHHS Office of Lean Management Services (OLMS) had its initial offices in a building that was in transition and was able to secure a large unused auditorium to use exclusively for working with improvement teams. This proved to very advantageous since it meant there was always space available controlled by OLMS. *BTC* used this space to create a Lean Lab, which provided room for teams to work together and ample wall space and whiteboards for mapping processes. The Lean Lab was used heavily during *BTC*'s start-up. Posters and VS maps could be left on the walls for periods of time and issues of scheduling space were no longer a problem. This room can be seen in operation in Figures 2 and 3.

Figure 2

In merging of the Department of Behavioral Health and the Department of Human Services, the new commissioner wanted to move OLMS to the DHHS Central Office headquarters building, which meant abandoning the Lean Lab. OLMS campaigned for Lean Lab space in its new quarters, using the work *BTC* was doing in the old auditorium as proof of concept. The new administration agreed that this space and service was value added to its operations and agreed to install a new Lean Lab, to *BTC's* specifications, in the Central Office, see Figures 4,5 and 6.

Figure 3

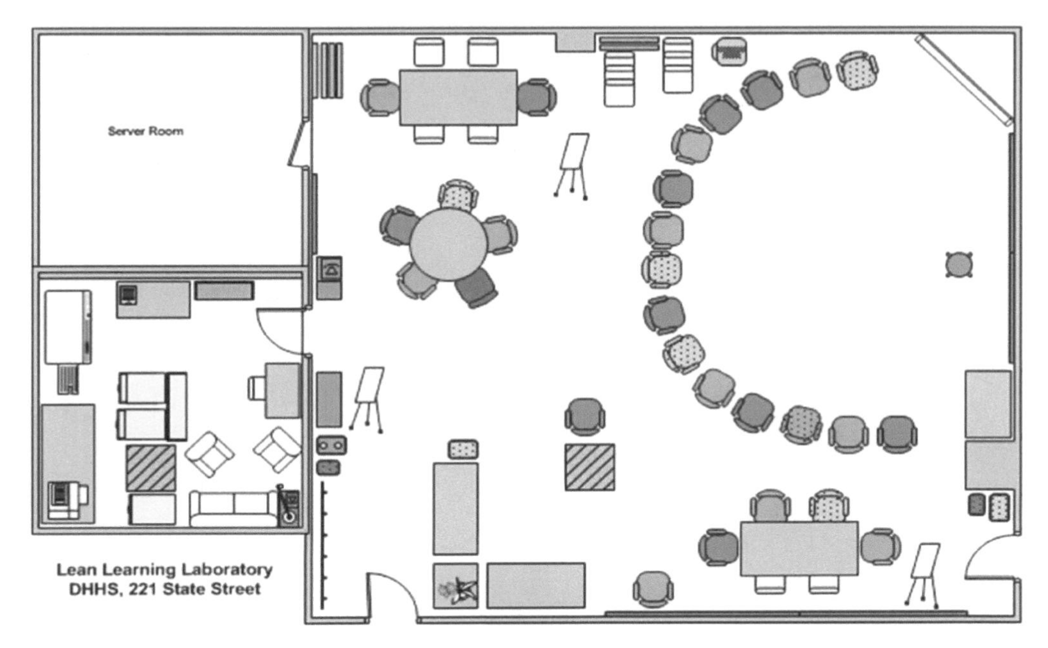

Figure 4
The Lean Lab Layout

The Lean Lab was approximately forty by fifty-five feet and as seen in Figure 4 contained a large meeting space where the improvement events were held and a small separate prep, consulting, and storage space that contained a copier, file cabinets, book shelves, a desk, and a couch and side chairs were available. Both rooms were wired with computer outlets. The main meeting room had twelve breakout tables and twenty-seven comfortable chairs; thus, it was versatile in how we could set it up. It was large enough so that with large teams of fifteen or more we could set up separate spaces to break the team down into smaller groups as needed. The walls had whiteboards running the length of them and could be used for putting up lengths of butcher paper for mapping processes. The general layout for VSM events is depicted in Figure 4. We always used a semicircle to work with teams with breakout tables off to the side. The round table in the back was used, as needed, for *BTC* observers. We also had flip charts and projectors available as necessary. Posters and other graphics were placed on the walls. Figure 5 and 6 depict an actual session in the Lean Lab.

Figure 5

Figure 6

The Lean Lab proved to be one of many unique innovations for *BTC*. Its primary goal was to relieve CIPs from the burden of constantly having to find and schedule space to do improvement work. Since *BTC* controlled the lab (with few exceptions), we were able to use the space exclusively for improvement work, which included preparing and planning for improvement events; doing actual improvement events, such as VSMs and other kaizen work; training; and a resource center for all things Lean in state government. The Lean Lab also became a key component of the *BTC* DOP and certification program, which we will detail in the next chapter.

Innovation comes from people who take joy in their work.
—W. Deming

CHAPTER 6: SUSTAINING *BTC*

This chapter discusses the challenge we faced sustaining *BTC* and the various strategies we developed to sustain Lean thinking in government and the long-term cultural change we were attempting in government. We sought to instill enough knowledge and capacity in state government so that we would no longer need expensive external consultants but instead build expert Lean knowledge into government culture. Elements of this CIP support structure are depicted in Figure 6.1 and discussed below.

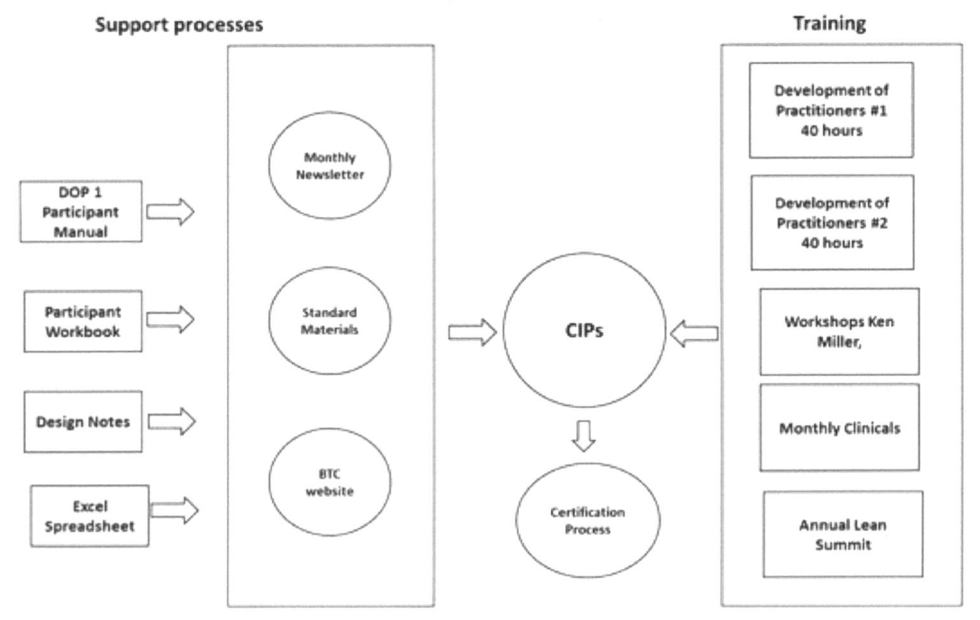

Figure 6.1—Support and Training Structure Design for *BTC*

CIP Selection: The purpose of developing the CIP role was to eventually eliminate the need for external consultants and to build into the fabric of government a capacity to continuously improve its own operations. CIPs were envisioned to "hold and disseminate" knowledge of Lean and continuous improvement and to be the in-house consultants, coaches, and mentors operating throughout government. The CIP role was also considered to be part of one's regular job responsibilities and not to be a separate job category.

Not surprisingly, we discovered that not anyone could be a CIP. The CIP responsibilities included a considerable knowledge and understanding of Lean and continuous improvement as well as skill in facilitating and leading people individually and in teams. This placed a premium on their time to do their assigned job functions, which required their supervisor to understand Lean and CI and its value to their organization in order to support the time commitment CIPs needed to be effective. Therefore, to be a CIP required a special individual able to meet the following:

- Is enthusiastic about the *BTC*/Lean principles, methods, techniques, and approach
- Has an ability, willingness, and enthusiasm for becoming a formal change agent in the *BTC* initiative
- Believes this work is a good investment of time and energy
- Can make the mandatory time commitment *and* participate fully with the following:
    - At least a two-year commitment
    - A minimum of thirty-six days a year for *BTC*/Lean activities, including those activities listed above
- Can make the commitment to fulfilling CI practitioner certification requirements
- Has full and strong management and supervisory support for doing this state of Maine and department-wide work
- Is willing and eager to learn, internalize, and apply new and sometimes challenging ideas and skills
- Can give and receive feedback
- Can demonstrate active listening skills
- Has good written and oral communication skills
- Can demonstrate a preference and willingness to use facts, or to learn to use facts, metrics, observations, and analysis versus guesses, assumptions, or expedient inferences/conclusions to prove a point

- Is comfortable with and has the ability (to learn) to lead/work effectively with diverse groups, preferably with some experience in working with groups
- Accepts the concept that development of self is core to leadership competency

In the eight years of its operation, *BTC* trained over seventy CIPs. Turnover rates were considerable with many of our trained CIPs leaving the practice either due to new job assignments in state government, leaving state government altogether, discovering that they did not have the time to commit to being a CIP, dropping out due to a discovery this was not something they wanted to do, or not having the skill level to be successful. *BTC* was committed to improving CIP practice by applying Lean/CI methods and principles to itself in order to enhance the knowledge and skill level and retention of its CIP cadre. In order to accomplish this, two initiatives were developed, a monthly training session called clinical supervision and a certification process. These two initiatives were put in place to provide ongoing training and skill development for CIPS to increase and enhance their practice and to sustain *BTC* in state government.

Monthly Clinicals: The purpose of the monthly clinical supervision was to provide a day-long training and discussion session for all CIPs who had gone through either the week-long development of practitioner (DOP1) and/or development of practitioner (DOP2) training sessions. The clinical was designed to provide a place to continue to learn *and* to practice the skills necessary to be effective CIPs. Clinical supervision was designed to provide a learning forum that would do the following:

- Deepen and broaden CI practitioners' competence and confidence in supporting process improvement teams to achieve successful outcome(s)
- Develop as a learning community in order to lead and support the development of the "CI practice" in state government within the context of transformational change
- Practice applying skills, knowledge, tools, concepts, and techniques in a "supervised" and safe environment

At these clinical sessions, training was usually offered in areas not covered in the introductory DOP training, instead providing practice and advanced training in skills and knowledge and opportunities to practice new skills and behaviors. At the very beginning of *BTC*, the clinicals were substantially led by the MDOL consultants, who were part of the leadership team for the first two years of *BTC*. Once the consultants' contracts were completed, CIPs assumed responsibility for the monthly clinical supervision sessions and continued this role throughout *BTC's* existence. Clinical supervision was considered a unique and value-added component of *BTC* (*as well as usually fun and very interesting*). Over time a standard agenda for the clinical was developed.

> Typical examples of Lean learnings included items such as: "Process Variation," "The DNA of Toyota," and "Henry Ford on Quality." Typical practice section items included: "Dental Process and Invoice Payment," "VSM Standard Process Review," and "Coaching and Development Plan."

Clinical Planning Committee: A clinical planning committee was created to plan and organize the agenda, topics, and presenters for the day-long monthly clinical sessions and was made up of certified CIPs and other CIPs interested in participating.

These volunteer CIPs were solicited and tasked with organizing and presenting various aspects of the clinical agenda. Clinical sessions used principles of adult learning to inform the delivery of content and case studies as the basis for the content. Case studies were often real-time and relevant. Cases were drawn from ongoing or completed VSMs, kaizen, or other continuous improvement teamwork. CIPs working with a team were responsible for developing cases to review and work on during a clinical session. Case studies for presentation and discussion at clinical were scheduled with the *BTC* clinical planning committee at least two weeks prior to the session, enabling staff and faculty to adequately prepare. Case studies were selected based on the content and the perceived needs of the practitioners. A standard format for the clinical is displayed below.

The morning session was primarily focused on Lean learnings, which included readings and articles of interest read by the attendees prior to the meeting. This was then followed by topics related to current CIP practice. The afternoon session included an open forum content which was decided on at the opening of the clinical in the morning and included special issues or topics or announcements CIPS wanted to discuss with the group; these items were prioritized and discussed during the time permitted. The open forum was then followed by a hands-on practice session and/or simulation where CIPs would have the opportunity to practice their skills and further their understanding of Lean and continuous improvement methods.

The Standard Agenda Developed for *BTC's* Clinical Supervision

Clinical Supervision

Clinical Purpose and Outcome:

- ✶ Increase CIPs' understanding of their consulting process
- ✶ Learn to question the obvious, the assumptions
- ✶ Continue to enhance our knowledge and development of the five competencies in our practice
- ✶ Understand and practice continuous improvement principles, methodologies, and tools

Agenda

8:15–8:30	**Welcome**
	Logistics
	Agenda Review
	Reminder: Cert. Matrix and Facilitation
	Volunteer for Scribe
	Announcements
8:30–8:45	**Check-in**
8:45–10:30	**Lean Learnings:** *Topic Name*
10:30–10:45	***Break***
10:45–12:00	**Practice:** *Topic Name*
12:00–1:00	***Lunch***
1:00–2:30	**Open Forum**
	FC: Topics and Time
	(Practice and Lean concerns, other questions and concerns, concepts, et cetera)
2:30–2:45	***Break***
2:45–4:15	**Lab:** *Session Name*
4:15–4:30	**Plan for Next Clinical**
	(*Sign-up for next clinical facilitation*)
	Check out and Adjourn

Certification Process. In addition to developing and sustaining a state Lean culture, one of the goals of Bend the Curve was to develop a cadre of "expert" practitioners who were skilled in the principles and methods of Lean and continuous improvement. As mentioned, most state employees at the inception of *BTC* had little to no knowledge of Lean or continuous improvement. Internal consultants at that time who had all the skills necessary to perform Lean and continuous improvement work in a state government setting were almost nonexistent, and there was virtually no organized training in Maine where we could send employees to get this type of training.

The development of practitioners' trainings (DOP1 and DOP2) were continuously redesigned and developed by the *BTC* leadership team.. They were comprehensive and provided a sound foundation for these principles and methods (see DOP windowpane). However, they could not provide enough of the hands-on practice needed by CIPs to become fully competent in working with state government improvement teams. As noted above, *BTC* had to modify an industrial Lean model to suit government work and then train CIPs in this model. CIP certification was *BTC's* answer to standardize CIP practice in a nonmanufacturing setting to assure that CIPs doing improvement work were fully capable of successfully working with the challenges of improving government and service operations.

Being a change agent and becoming a CIP were challenging endeavors, and ongoing training and development were as necessary as they were important. To be certified as a continuous improvement practitioner, candidates were expected to actively continue their development beyond their DOP training and their process improvement practice in order to advance and develop their skills.

Developing a Certification Process: Early in *BTC's* development, the consultants and the Lean leadership teams from MDOL and DHHS met to plan and develop a certification process that would be rigorous enough to assure the capability of CIPs. The certification process included a mix of practice and skill development, enhanced knowledge and expertise in Lean and continuous improvement, an examination, and a portfolio that would document a CIP's practice and experience. CIPs were assigned a certified CIP to assist in meeting the requirements for certification. The initial mentoring and certification fell to the consultants since at the time *BTC* did not have anyone certified. Once a few CIPs became certified, they served as mentors for other CIPs seeking certification. The following list details the requirements that all CIP practitioners were expected to meet to be certified. During the development of the certification process, we reviewed other certification processes, and envisioned three levels of certification for our CIPs: bronze, silver, and gold. These are displayed in Figure 6.2 below. *BTC* developed the first level, bronze, below, reflecting the level I certification process and the several mastery levels.

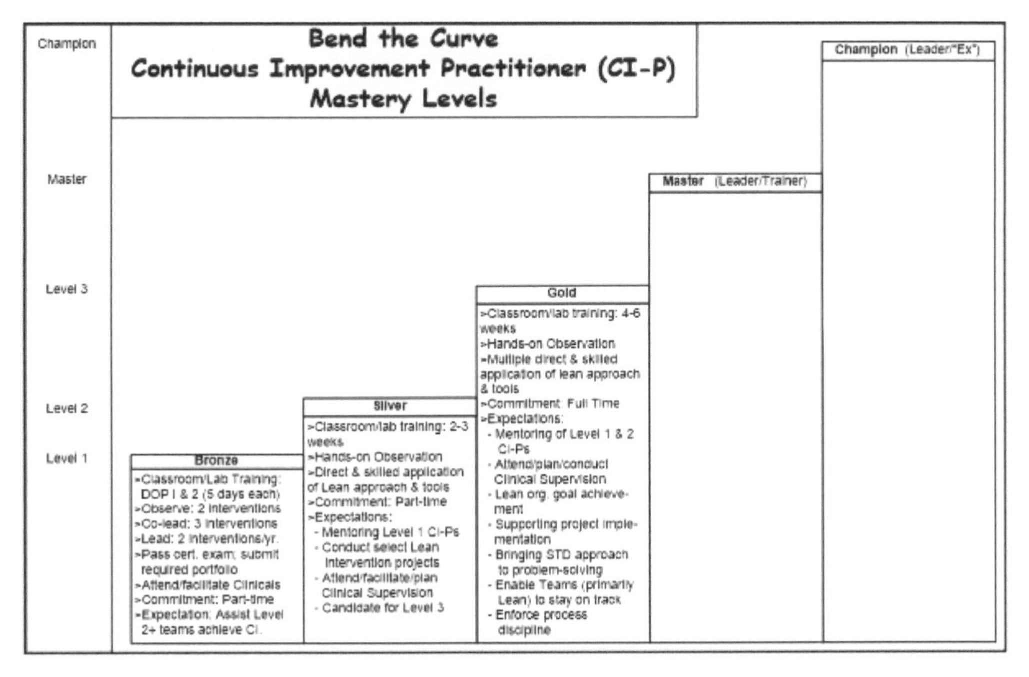

Figure 6.2

CIP Certification Requirements: To be certified as a continuous improvement practitioner at the bronze level of mastery, candidates were expected to continue their development and engage in process improvement/change activities to advance and develop their skills. The following Figure 6.3 and the list outline the requirements that all practitioners were required to meet to be certified:

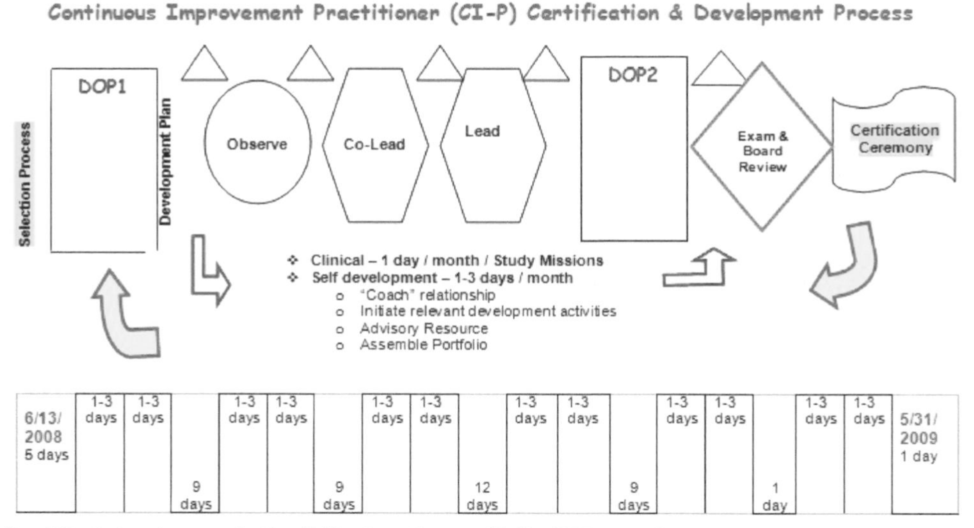

Figure 6.3

- Attend and successfully complete the initial, introductory five-day CI practitioner training program
- Attend clinical supervision group sessions at least one full day a month, with an overall 80 percent attendance
- Actively participate in Bend the Curve fairs/conventions/et cetera
- Attend and successfully complete advanced/enhanced trainings, including DOP2, as required
- Participate fully in Bend the Curve/Lean/continuous improvement activities
- Facilitate VSMs, from chartering through documentation and implementation, observing two VSMs, co-leading two VSMs and one kaizen, and leading 2 VSMs
- Complete and pass the bronze level exam with at least 90 percent accuracy
- Demonstrate an acceptable skill level in all the identified competencies (observed and documented by certified CIP)
- Submit a complete and approved portfolio
- Evidence a working knowledge of how the measurements are calculated and applied throughout the process

Certification TimeLine: A typical timeline for a CIP to meet certification requirements involved an employee first applying to attend a *BTC*-sponsored week-long (forty hours) development of practitioners' session. These sessions were offered on average once or twice a year. The candidate would be required to be sponsored by their department manager and have an improvement project they would work on after they completed the DOP. After completing the DOP, the CIP would then work on the project back at the work site under the supervision of a certified CIP and eventually be assigned to a VSM or improvement event as an observer. The CIP would be expected to attend with the lead and co-lead all planning sessions for the VSM (including the initial meeting with the sponsor) and attend design note sessions with the lead and co-lead CIPs to observe and learn how to prepare for a VSM or other kaizen events. Design sessions generally took four to eight hours for each day of the improvement event. The CIP observers were then expected to attend and observe for the duration of the actual event. A standardized observation sheet was given to the CIP to make notes on what he or she observed or had questions about during the improvement event. This regimen was repeated a second time for the CIP after which the CIP was assigned as co-lead for two improvement events. As a co-lead, the CIP was under the supervision and mentorship of the certified lead CIP and was assigned components of the improvement event as agreed upon and designated in the design notes for that event. Generally, by the second assigned event, the learning CIP was given a more significant role in the event. The rationale for this whole training process was to ensure that the CIP in training can work independently and at a high level of performance on an improvement event using this standard model.

In addition to the above, the additional requirements leading to certification were as follows:

- Each DOP must result in a development plan for the practitioner. A coach/mentor has accountability to support the practitioner to follow through in some way. DOP2 usually occurs about six months after a DOP1.
- The portfolio must be submitted at least two weeks prior to certification review and include the following:
    - Documents supporting the completion of steps in the appropriate level of CIP development; evidence of observation and co-lead and lead CIP develop process (VSM charters, any final reports such as an A3, maps, implementation plans, documented outcomes, et cetera)
        - Written success/failure story—the lessons learned, key learnings from the work
        - Observation sheets

- Evidence of development of competencies (observed and completed by certified CIP)
- Letter of recommendation from coach/mentor
- Evidence of written exam completed and passed

Summary of CIP Certification Milestones: In order to be certified at the first (bronze) of the mastery levels, the CIP must at least successfully do the following:

- Observe: two complete interventions (minimum one VSM and one kaizen)
- Learning Co-lead: three complete interventions (minimum two VSMs and one kaizen)
- Learning Lead: two complete VSMs
- Pass certification exam
- Complete DOP1 and DOP2
- Be observed by certified CIP and meet competencies/standards
- Submit complete CIP portfolio
- Attend 80 percent of clinical supervisions in prior six months

The CIP checklist and certification exam is found in the appendix. D and E.

Study Missions: As part of the *BTC's* clinical supervision, study missions (going to the *gemba*) to businesses and companies practicing Lean were conducted for the purpose of enabling CIPs to see and learn from Lean principles and methods in operation in settings other than government. This was a practical and deliberate attempt to expand the knowledge base and confidence of CIPs that Lean works in a variety of different settings, to see and understand that Lean principles and methods are universal.

These were not seen as field trips but as "study missions" with a standardized protocol that included a standard baseline set of questions that were assigned to attendees to answer as they toured a particular plant. A copy of the study mission protocol can be found in appendix F. These questions were then used in a debrief session after the study. Study mission observations and notes were then collated and published in *BTC's* monthly

Study Mission Schedule
Leave at 7:30
Travel time at one hour
Study Mission at 9:00 to 12:00

- Organizational Overview
- *Gemba* Walk
- Discussion, Q&A

Lunch at 12:00–1:45 (if appropriate)
Travel Time at one hour
Debriefs

- *Team Study Mission Debrief*
- *Clinical Debrief*

CIP Newsletter (to be discussed below). A typical study mission agenda is set forth in the side bar.

Study missions were primarily undertaken in warm weather months with an average attendance between six and twelve people. The organization to be visited set the maximum number of participants each preferred. Generally, we traveled as a group in a state van. This made for a good team-building activity and allowed for a debrief, and often we stopped on the way home for lunch. These study missions proved to be very rewarding and "eye opening" for CIPs, who looked forward to them.

Website: *BTC* developed a web page that was linked to the state of Maine's DHHS public website. The purpose of the site was to provide a useful and easily accessible source of information to CIPs and other interested personnel on the activities of Bend the Curve. The page included links to Lean reference articles and books, current *BTC* activities, summaries of improvement events, and a listing of all standardized forms and documents that CIPs used in their work with customers. The *BTC* page was accessible outside the state's fire wall, and we found that it was used extensively by other Lean practitioners around the country with frequent requests to download items. The standardized forms that *BTC* developed over the years attracted other state Lean initiatives that were interested in using or modifying them for use within their respective practices. Since these materials were developed with public funds, they were available for public use, provided an acknowledgment to the source was noted.

Outreach: As *BTC's* reputation and activities evolved, *BTC* received requests from external organizations seeking to send their employees to the development of practitioner (DOP1) training. These entities included other state departments, hospitals, out-of-state government organizations, and even out-of-country (Canada). These requests for training were honored, and they were charged the standard fee for each attendee. These "out-of-network" organizations helped to spread Lean ideas beyond immediate Maine state government with the intent of further strengthening the relationship to local community organizations struggling to improve and prosper. It also provided another forum for *BTC* to learn and benefit from what other organizations, states, and countries were doing.

> At one of our early awareness sessions, for example, in which the governor was in attendance, Jim Womack's book *Lean Thinking* was on the desk in front of him, and we when he saw it he thought that this was something to do with dieting! Unfortunately, not unusual.

The Annual Lean Summit: At the time of *BTC* inception, there was little understanding of Lean in and outside of state government. There were a few manufacturing companies in the state that were starting Lean programs and supported by the state's local MEP, but for the most part there were few. As *BTC* evolved it became critical that our legislative and executive leaders understood the power that Lean thinking could bring to government operations. In order to expand support and understanding of these ideas, *BTC* decided to plan a summit in the summer to bring together government and private and public business sectors interested in or implementing Lean methods and practices in order to share knowledge and successes. This became an annual affair starting in the summer of 2010 and became known as the Lean Systems Summit held each August in Portland, Maine.

Its purpose is as follows:

- To establish a Lean network in Maine that promotes and supports Lean practice in business and government
- To create a business climate that reflects modern management practices that are efficient and effective, customer focused, and centered on the tools and methodology of Lean/CI principles and methods
- Inform business and government leaders of the importance of applying Lean methods and practices in a global economy
- Highlight companies where Lean methods and practice are successful

A small working group of volunteers in 2009 worked to put the Lean summit in place. This group became known as the Continuous Improvement Lean Collaborative (CILC) and consists of a multistate network of public and private individuals, organizations, and companies interested and involved in Lean and continuous improvement. Its goal is to provide a forum for practitioner and organizational learning, active collaboration, and sharing of knowledge, experience, and resources across all sectors.

The collaborative's leadership has included representatives of Jotul North America; state/provincial governments of Maine, New Hampshire, New Brunswick, and Connecticut; Lonza Rockland; Town of Durham, New Hampshire; IDEXX Laboratories, Inc.; Maine Manufacturing Extension Partnerships; Infinite Services, Inc.; Lean Capitol, LLC, and New Hampshire's New Futures.

The Lean Systems Summit has now evolved into a two-day conference with the first day designed to provide in-depth training on Lean/CI topics. The second day includes three keynote speakers and provides shorter presentations on a variety of topics. The scope of the summit is to provide a place where government, services, and manufacturing meet. The summit provides an excellent opportunity to exchange experiences, ideas, and knowledge about all things Lean. It is also a place to network and increase knowledge of Lean continuous improvement and its application to the workplace. The Lean summit is preparing for its tenth year as of this writing and has proven to be one of the most enduring elements of the *BTC* legacy.

CIP Newsletter: As part of its ongoing support for its CIP cadre, *BTC* developed a CIP newsletter, which was published monthly. The newsletter contained news of interest to CIPs, ongoing improvement issues in government, the status of CIP activities, and training schedules and opportunities. The CIP newsletter was published monthly for the last six years of *BTC* operations and was available online during this time.

We can do something about our problems,
or we can continue the way we are.
—W. Edwards Deming

CHAPTER 7: IMPROVEMENT INTERVENTIONS AND RESULTS

This chapter provides a summary of *BTC* results during the years of its operation. These results include an overall assessment of the impact of *BTC* on Maine state government, acknowledging that our assessment is subjective since we were not able to do a full-scale evaluation of the *BTC* program. We present these results from both a quantitative and qualitative perspective. They include concrete improvements that were documented as well as observations of behavioral changes in staff that participated in improvement events sponsored by *BTC*.

One of the main goals of Bend the Curve was to change how state employees perceived and approached their work from an improvement perspective (i.e., to change the culture of the state government workforce). There has been much written in the Lean literature about changing an organization's culture, pointing to two general themes: (1) changing behaviors—what do people do differently in the workplace—and (2) changing mindsets—how do they think differently about work. Both of which are intimately connected.

The scope of *BTC* was limited to a handful of state departments over approximately eight years. Seeing a dramatic change in government operations, particularly without the full support of the executive, was at best difficult. What we did see, though, was a continued and sustained interest and support in midlevel management and line staff, which was demonstrated in several ways as follows:

- Recognition that *BTC's* Lean methods worked as evidenced by management continuing to access *BTC* services throughout the eight years
- Repeated use of *BTC* services by the same managers who saw the value of *BTC* and continued to rely on *BTC* to assist with improvement efforts throughout their respective departments/offices
- The initial ongoing support of senior management at the commissioner level to use *BTC* as a tool for improving work processes
- The change in language that management and staff used to describe work in terms of value added and waste
- The ongoing ability of *BTC* to recruit new CIPs both from multiple state departments—other than just DHHS and MDOL—as well as staff from external entities including hospitals, universities, and out-of-state municipal government.

Translating Lean to Government: One of the unique and initial challenges *BTC* faced was discovering how to present Lean principles and methods in a government environment. Lean carries with it a lot of unnecessary and negative baggage, not the least of which is the idea that Lean is often interpreted to mean "less employees are needed." When introduced to Maine state government, Lean, if known at all, was perceived in a negative light, as if it were designed to reduce the number of employees, and thus resistance to its deployment was felt by *BTC* sponsors. To offset this concern, *BTC* did get a commitment from our respective commissioners that no employees would lose their jobs as a result of Lean improvement efforts. These commitments were broadcast widely to staff along with the idea that state employees were already overwhelmed with work and that any jobs that were freed up from Lean initiatives would be reassigned to other positions and/or as part of the attrition process. CIPs consistently emphasized that Lean afforded staff the opportunity to help improve their work by making it better and less stressful for them and more valued by their customers.

We believe one measure of *BTC's* success was the reengineering of standard Lean manufacturing strategies to approaches that enabled state employees to easily understand them and to see their work differently. The strategies and approaches that translated manufacturing concepts and methods into a language that government and service sector employees could easily grasp was one of *BTC's* greatest successes. Many of these methods and strategies were published on the *BTC* website and were used by other states in developing their Lean programs.

Scope of *BTC* in Maine State Government: Most of the improvement work occurred in two state departments: the Departments of Labor and the Department of Health and Human Services. We estimated that there were hundreds of work processes in each of the respective departments. Overall *BTC* worked on approximately seventy. There were a variety of different types of work processes that CIPs completed, including clinical services, administrative services, finance, HR operations, grant writing, and IT services, to name a few. As word spread about the success *BTC* was having with improvement work, other departments in addition to DHHS and MDOL asked *BTC* for improvement help. These included the Departments of Education, Transportation, Financial and Administrative Affairs, and Marine Resources as well as DHHS MaineCare (Maine's version of Medicare) and Public Health and the Office of Information Technology. CIPs helped facilitate important work in all of them. As the knowledge of the *BTC* program spread around the state, CIPs were also asked to support the University of Southern Maine, a local hospital, and a municipal government from a neighboring state.

The Numbers: A typical *BTC* improvement event consisted of three CIPs (one lead facilitator, a co-lead, and one or more observers) along with an improvement team ranging in size from ten to as many as twenty-five members, although we generally sought to work with no more than twelve participants. The net results of this activity for MDOL and DHHS meant that *BTC* trained seventy-eight CIPs who led or assisted in the eight years of *BTC's* operations over seventy process improvement events with a minimum of over 1,050 state employees. Total savings for MDOL was estimated at $12,329,163.00 with an average savings of $269,537.00. For DHHS, the savings totaled $5,189,097.00 with an average savings per improvement event of $128,951.00. In most cases, the average estimated savings for each improvement could in fact be carried over for each subsequent year after the improvement was completed. Table 7.1 summarizes these findings for *BTC*, for both MDOL and DHHS.

Table 7.1

Department	Events	Total Savings[1]	Average Savings[2]	Five Year Impact[3]
MDOL	39	$39,201,606	$269,537.00	$1,347,685.00
DHHS	37	$5,189,097.00	$128,951.00	$644,755.00
Totals	**70**	**$17,318,260.00**	**$199,244.00**	**$1,992,440**

[1] Total estimated savings from 2006 through 2008

[2] Average saving per event

[3] Per process

Table 8.1 does not capture all the gains and benefits that *BTC* contributed to the state government but rather reflects data reported and available to us at the time. Of the seventy events, there was a wide range in savings per improvement event, ranging from several thousand dollars to several million dollars. Savings reported in Table 7.1 are estimated gains by the improvement teams if all the improvements identified were completed. We know that in some cases improvement teams were not able to achieve all of the identified improvements, and hence, the total is estimated gains. Nonetheless, the overall potential benefit to the state was significant considering (1) that executive management supported but did not drive *BTC* improvement efforts (unlike the TQM era when the governor chaired a monthly Quality Improvement Council with report-outs from every state department) and (2) how few improvements were completed given the many hundreds, if not thousands, of business processes that existed in government.

These estimates were based on staff time savings, which were the difference in time between current and future state conditions. As mentioned above we used fifty-eight cents per minute as an average cost for a state employee (see chapter 6). The amount of staff time available for a state employee is set forth in the sidebar. These numbers were used in calculating cost savings based on available staff time saved, the difference between current and future states.

Staff Time calculations
State Hour = 50 Minutes
State Day = 400 Minutes
State Year = 220 Days = 88,000 Minutes
3,866,244/88,000 = 43.9, or 44 FTE

In addition to cost savings, other benefits were accrued in the following areas: delivery time, error reduction, reallocation of resources to mission critical areas, and customer and staff satisfaction. In every improvement event, *BTC* saw gains in some if not all these areas. It became a matter of course that CIPs could "*guarantee*" that the improvement team would be able to identify and improve their processes, not surprising since employees always have ideas for improvement if given the forum to address them. The biggest challenge in achieving these improvements always rested with the sponsor and value stream manager being committed to following through with the identified improvements.

One of the major success stories of *BTC* during its operation was the work done by the Health and Environmental Testing Lab (HETL). The director of HETL saw the value of Lean and devoted considerable time in using *BTC* resources to totally transform the health lab. This work began with a visioning process and ended with value stream mapping and 5S activity in all the major labs in the facility. HETL became a focal point for study missions for state staff, managers, and legislators to see the value of Lean in government. The commentary below is based on a report by the lab manager on the work that was done using Lean and *BTC* resources.

The Health and Environmental Testing Laboratory (HETL): The Division of Public Health Systems of the Maine Center for Disease and Control in the Department of Health and Human Services had underdone significant changes with its management, staff, revenue sources, physical structure, new technologies, and partners in public health. As these changes were occurring within the HETL lab; significant changes were also occurring within the larger organizational structure. Early in the DHS/DHHS merger, HETL management believed that the approach used to create governing principles might be very helpful to the laboratory. The HETL desired alignment with the strategic plans of the MeCDC and DHHS to be based upon these guiding principles. Realizing that strategic plans are about outcomes, the HETL believed that the process used to achieve outcomes must capture the unique culture of the laboratory environment. The Lean principles and methods of the Bend the Curve program were the journey that the HETL chose to begin the process of change.

The Lean journey began with the HETL seeking the assistance of a lead CIP, who helped articulate and refine the values, goals, and objectives the HETL was trying to achieve. A new management team was formed within the lab to develop and then build upon the core foundational values developed by the laboratory staff. These values and guiding principles became the foundation for change management. This process included a laboratory-wide SWOT (strengths, weaknesses, opportunities, threats) analysis, with these results posted in the HETL. Lean training flowed directly from these initiatives. The process orientation of the Bend the Curve program seemed a natural fit with the HETL's commitment to improve its efficiency in working with limited resources. Senior management attended a multisession course on Lean and continuous improvement. Section teams were trained and then developed value stream mapping (VSM) charters and completed VSMs. Significant savings of resources were identified, but most importantly, staff became the driving force behind ideas for improvement and the elimination of waste. The support of the Lean process was one of the reasons that the HETL volunteered to take part in a national performance standard project by the Association of Public Health Laboratories to measure quality improvement as a public health partner. HETL was honored by the association with the Performance Standard Pioneer Award for leadership in initiating quality improvement for the state public health system. This included a thorough review of lab processes and improvement and involved many steps. The lab director and many staff members undertook this project as a means of independent review of recent improvements due to the incorporation of Lean production management.

Realizing that this is a long-term journey, the HETL's significant achievement was the high level of participation of staff at all levels within the organization. The process was very time-consuming, involving significant training. One surprise was that staff who initially expressed disapproval and cynicism as we began the Lean journey often surprisingly changed their attitude after participation in a VSM. The VSM charters identify leaders within the organization whose commitment is important to its success. One observation was that the VSM process success was augmented significantly by the CIPs who skillfully sought staff participation.

The biggest downside to the process to both the buy-in of staff and the success the lab experienced was that inefficiencies in other parts of state government were now easily noticed. Lab staff realized the importance of extending the Lean philosophy to other outside entities. Typically, staff was concerned that "we need to continuously ask permission to do our job" as staff was looking at management to lead with "yes" rather than "no." As an example, IT was a partner that the lab needed most to perform its job, since data is the lab's product. Within the lab, silos and barriers were broken down, and there was more teamwork and more interest in visual measures, order, and efficiency. The roles of management and leadership evolved, and staff understood the challenges to management to implement tools like 5S, standup meetings, process flow, visual controls, and standard work. The lab director clearly saw his role as a leader that creates change and as a team member that often works *for* the staff. Below is one example of an improvement event undertaken by the HETL to improve the inventory control and ordering process, which includes VS maps and results.

Description: The Health and Environmental Testing Laboratory orders and purchases laboratory equipment, expendable materials, offices supplies, and services as necessary to perform and report laboratory analyses of clinical, environmental and forensic samples.

Problems to Solve:

1. Lack of effective cost-accounting and efficient materials management due to -
   a. inability to retrieve appropriate data from the State purchasing system and
   b. absence of an integrated laboratory accounting system (including a general ledger, purchasing, receiving and inventory).
2. Lack of standardized ordering across lab sections, promoting errors and inefficient use of personnel.
3. Redundant purchases from different lab sections.
4. Poorly visible order and disbursement codes so that HETL Receiving cannot easily distinguish the requestor.

Improvement Team:

Sponsor - CZL, KP

Manager - Ken & Tom
Staff Members - Lisa , Jason , James, Chris, Lori, Julie, Brian, Veronica, Cori

CI-Ps - Walter, Lita

Maine CDC Health & Environmental Laboratory (HETL) Inventory Control & Ordering

Identify needed supplies & equipment ... Order supplies & equipment ... Receive supplies & equipment ... Pay invoice

Prompted by cost-accounting and inventory control concerns, Maine CDC HETL staff began concerted work to improve their inventory control & ordering process using a continuous improvement approach. With the assistance of the Office of Lean Management, the team mapped their current process on January 7, 2010; created a new future process on February 3rd; and, on the 10th, identified the changes and actions needed to put the improved process in place, which it is actively implementing.

The following major change strategies for improving inventory control and ordering have been recommended by the Team:

A. Enhance resources needed for improvement implementation.
B. Enhance/Improve current process regardless of additional resources/funding availability.
C. Streamline Order Entry in order to eliminate duplicate data entry and tracking and improve accuracy.
D. Define business requirements in order to develop specifications for inventory and ordering software system.
E. Research & implement appropriate HETL single Software System.
F. Streamline Approval processes.
G. Streamline identification and centralization/sharing of changes in ordering information.
H. Streamline Common Inventory Control & Area.
I. Define standard inventory ordering information & process to stream-line the ordering process and assure its timeliness & accountability.

TOTAL PROCESS TIMES for an order		
Current Process		
Non-Federal/Funds Available:	Work Time 3h 12m – 6h 49m	
	Elapsed Time 3d 12h 12m – 148d 10h 40m	
Non-Federal/Funds Not Available:	Work Time 3h 18m – 6h 4m	
	Elapsed Time 3d 12h – 182d 9h 10m	
For Federal Order, Add:	Work Time 11m-1h 6m	Elapsed Time 2d 2h – 52d
$5,000+ Order, Add:	Work Time 2m-8m	Elapsed Time 6h-12d
Future Process		
Funds Available:	Work Time 31m – 3h 19m	
	Elapsed Time 5d 2h 45m – 29d 15h 37m	
Funds Not Available:	Work Time 33m – 3h 15m	
	Elapsed Time 4d 1h 4m – 11w 15h 37m	
$5,000+ Order, Add:	Work Time 1m-3m	Elapsed Time 4h-7d
Projected Savings per order (@ $0.58/minute, fully-burdened, staff work time)		
Funds Available:	Work Time $93 -- $122	Elapsed Time Improvement 46% (+) -- 80%
Funds Not Available:	Work Time $96 -- $98	Elapsed Time Improvement 16% (+) -- 57%
$5,000+ Order, Add:	Work Time $0.58 -- $3	Elapsed Time Improvement 33% -- 42%
Annual Volume: 10-18,000 per order/per vendor/per contract-agreement		

Improvement Initiatives: Using common conventions and standards enabled improvement project results to be compared for improvement initiatives and their summaries and reports. For example, use of a standard convention to convert state staff time saved to money—fully burdened cost—computed at an average fifty-eight centers per minute. Resulted in the use of 12 percent attrition as opposed to layoffs, reflecting a longer-range view with MDOL being the only state department that did not lay off staff. *BTC* documented $16 million in savings.

Improvement Project Teams. Below are selected examples of some of the improvement interventions.

Process	Description	Delivery Time Improvement	Savings
Adoption Services (AS)	The adapted design of this intervention included conduct of CS mapping sessions in each of the eight Maine district offices throughout June and July 2006. These eight maps were brought together by a representative department wide AS team on July 25 into a common statewide current state. The next day, the team went on to develop the new, standardized AS future process. By early August 2006, the team produced its improvement action plan. Process improvements included: Shorter time to permanency. Standardization of procedures/ practice. Combining of steps in the new process. Elimination of some steps. Different ways of approaching challenges.	40 percent	$124,166
Allocation Plans and Work Programs	Allocation plans are rarely completed on time and often contain significant errors or omissions. This problem results in poorly constructed work programs and departmental budgets, which create allotment issues that necessitate financial orders and delay payments to vendors.	85 percent reduction in lead time.	$656,625

Central Office Adult MR Waiver Funding Review	Process: Central Office review and approval of regional funding requests for new or additional services for people receiving services from the MR home and community-based waiver. Presently, there is a weekly central review and approval of regional funding requests for new or additional services for people receiving or wishing to receive services from the adult mental retardation home and community-based waiver program. The existing process is tedious, duplicates effort and steps, requires enormous paper shuffling, and frustrates all those "customers" who come in contact with it, for a variety of reasons. In order to address this, a team of five adult mental retardation staff, along with two facilitators, participated in a three-and-one-half-day process improvement session, utilizing Lean principles.	The recommended changes, when implemented as planned, would result in projected annual savings of $73,476, a 74 percent decrease in staff time, and a 133 percent increase in efficiency in the proposed future state process.	$73,476
Death Certificate Filing and Closure	The complex Maine CDC vital statistics death certificate filing and closure process needed to be significantly streamlined, as well as responsive to policy changes and high customer demands with decreasing resources.	Reduced customer lead time from ninety days to five days and reduced the number of processing steps from twenty-three to eleven. Customers of this process have given many praises to vital stats for the improved timeliness in acquiring death certificates from the state of Maine. 12.09: An automated process is scheduled to be	

		implemented, which has the potential to reduce the lead time to seconds.	
HETL Environmental Chemistry Section Workflow	Environmental testing involves a complex workflow due in part to the need to test multiple analytes on a single sample. Complex instrumentation is vulnerable to uptime issues and IT problems create rework. This work process takes place across multiple management sections of the laboratory, and the process is not yet fully visible or standardized. We aim to visualize the workflow in this section in order to make improvements that will reduce lead time, improve uptime, and reduce rework.	90 percent reduction in lead time.	$102,973
Accessioning HETL Microbiology	Reduce lead time for samples accessioning, simplify the workflow, and reduce rework.	90 percent reduction in lead time.	$120,582
HETL Supplies Ordering and Inventory Control	The Health and Environmental Testing Laboratory orders and purchases laboratory equipment, expendable materials, and office supplies and services as necessary to perform and report laboratory analyses of clinical, environmental, and forensic samples.	99 percent reduction in lead time.	$44,225
Accounts Receivable and Collections Process	There are inconsistencies and possibly inefficiencies in how we receive and handle monies (primarily checks) in this process.	99 percent reduction in time to process check receivables	NA
DHHS-OIAS Bangor **Eligibility Review**	A key element of the OIAS eligibility process is completion of the annual review of eligibility. The accuracy and completeness of the review is a critical part of the overall	46 percent reduction in lead time.	$377,080

	quality of the client case record and directly impacts case error rate—more specifically, the food stamp error rate. This VSM examined the eligibility review process and identified improvements and efficiencies that could be made. This would improve customer service but also target specific areas that are vulnerable to error. The VSM process identified ways to mitigate these errors and identify best practices that lead to accurate eligibility determinations and timely completion of case actions.		
Invoicing Process VSM	Invoicing the correct project with accurate staff time. There are 240 accounts and 150 staff. Accounts change from month to month. The existing process is tedious, duplicates effort and steps, requires enormous paper shuffling, and frustrates all those "customers" who touch it for a variety of reasons. It is error prone, untimely, and leads to inaccuracies in the whole accounting process.	82 percent reduction in lead time.	$102,973
Payroll Process	Processing payroll statewide has become a challenge for state departments for the following reasons: • Underutilization of staff • No backup systems • Errors resulting in inaccurate payments • Inadequate internal controls • Bottlenecks within the process (e.g., merit increases)	82 percent reduction in lead time	$19,822.00

	While some progress has been made with updated technologies, it is necessary to continue integrating statewide payroll services to provide the ability to share resources across agencies as well as improve services for all employees.		
Infectious Disease Surveillance	Refined the process of infectious disease reporting, registration, investigation, confirmation, and efficiency.	82 percent reduction in lead time	$1,571,638

Culture Changes: We saw the following as a move toward culture change in how state employees perceived their work:

- **The development of a shared Lean language.** A shared language is key to a culture. Staff participating in CIP-facilitated improvement events were introduced to the language of Lean—value, workflow, process, waste, et cetera—and began to use this language and apply it to their daily work—that government does have processes, does have customers, does have products, and does affect outcomes for its customers. Staff were exposed to and understood the concept of *waste*, the concept of *value-added*, and that a problem is an opportunity for improvement.
- **An understanding that improving one's work is part of one's work and Lean principles and methods work**. This was reflected in increased participation in continuous improvement events/projects, continued interest and participation in the DOPs, and increased attention/requests from state managers outside the founding departments of MDOL and DHHS.

  As one State employee explained, "Integration of Lean principles has been incorporated into our day-to-day work, decision-making, analysis with staff automatically identifying waste or redundant/unnecessary activity. As a matter of course, some of are beginning to work these concepts into our creation of new processes so that we start out more efficiently than we may have before."
- **Use of a disciplined problem-solving approach and development of process mindset.** Staff began to understand that problems are the result of processes, not people. It was not uncommon for staff to become excited to see their work process mapped out and to recognize that the problems

they were experiencing were system problems that they could identify and begin to alleviate.

- **Increasing use of, demand for, and reliance on qualitative and quantitative data in planning and making decisions.** Making changes based on facts/data rather than emotion. Staff saw a value stream map as an important tool to operationally describe and quantity their work. They also began to understand why other change efforts often made things worse not better and that making changes to work without understanding it from a process/system perspective was a concrete example of what Deming called "tampering."
- **A legitimization of the expectation that the persons doing the work, providing the services, and using government's services and products must be part of planning and decision-making.** Managers' increasing willingness to commit staff and teams to do the improvement work.
- **Increased awareness of Lean principles and methods in the government and service sectors.** This was evidenced by:
    - The numbers of CIPs (seventy-eight trained) and *BTC* participants (over one thousand)
    - Multistate collaboration and recognition
    - Use of our materials by other entities
    - An emerging shared Lean language
    - Expressed interest by Maine's gubernatorial candidates
    - Engagement with other public sector entities, such as the University of Maine, and savings/gains/benefits realized. Much of the work of *BTC* was reflected in the results of the improvements made by *BTC* and the programs and agencies.
- **Increasing acceptance of Lean continuous improvement as a legitimate and deliberate way of making improvements.** Throughout the eight years of *BTC's* operation, many managers came to see *BTC* and its Lean methods as a significant resource to help them and their department to make lasting improvements. It was mentioned above that it was not uncommon for the same manager to use the *BTC* to work on several of their department's processes. In at least one case, a departmental manager, described above, used *BTC* to reengineer his entire department. *BTC* was also seen as a useful way to develop new business processes, and it was frequently the case that CIPs were asked to help facilitate the development of them using Lean principles and methods.

Maine government is geographically dispersed over a large area, and it was often the case that the same government work processes, the adoption of children as an example, operated differently in different field offices, which caused confusion for staff, citizens, and management. These proved to be prime areas for developing standard work but with the challenge of assuring front-line staff from different offices were included in the improvement effort. These types of challenges were readily solved by CIPs by keeping the principle of "staff doing the work know the problems" front and center and designing the improvement efforts to include them wherever they worked.

You do not install quality; you begin to work at it.
—W. Edwards Deming

CHAPTER 8: SUMMARY AND LESSONS LEARNED

Bend the Curve sought to address the following:

- **Changing Service Demands and Resource Levels**. Increasing and more complex service demands and decreasing resources demanded greater governmental efficiencies and effectiveness.
- **Transformation of a Command and Control Culture.** Historically, government has sustained a culture and structure that are generally hierarchical—not responsibility based—promoting control, power, privilege, and organizational silos.
- **Perception of Government**. Citizens perceive that government operations are wasteful, with confidence in government responsiveness eroding steadily over time.

BTC faced three major challenges: (1) Lean was exclusively a manufacturing approach, (2) civil servants were unaccustomed to viewing themselves in terms of customer-supplier-production dynamics; and (3) previous quality improvement initiatives had "failed." *BTC's* intent was to transform how work is done in government through the following:

a) Internal Capacity: *BTC* trained an internal "volunteer" interdepartmental team of continuous improvement practitioners (CIPs) in Lean and other process/system improvement principles and methods. Over seventy CIPs were eventually trained.

b) Adapting a Manufacturing Model to Government: Translating Lean methodology and tools to a government environment. Extensive materials were developed and hosted on the state's *BTC* website.

c) Continuous Development: *BTC* applied continuous improvement approaches to its ongoing program development, including personnel, strategies, materials, and a structure for required and other special trainings/workshops, monthly day-long clinicals, study missions, and a certification process.

d) Interdepartmental Commitment: Originally unplanned, this was a natural consequence of learning and practicing Lean concepts and providing Lean consulting assistance to many other state government departments.

e) Introduction of Value Stream Mapping and Kaizen Approaches to Government: Innovative team-based problem-solving—making work visible enabled staff to align goals, share knowledge, and see and improve their work.

f) Developing a holistic implementation model: *BTC* developed an implementation strategy that brought together Lean/continuous improvement principles and practices and organization development knowledge and strategies. This recognized that it is as much about the hearts and minds of individuals as it is their technical skills and knowledge.

Results and Policy Impact: Despite the obstacles mentioned above, one of the most significant, rewarding achievements of *BTC* was the difficult and slow but noticeably emerging change we saw in the culture of state government. Although Lean principles and methodologies have been around for decades, transformation was fitful and slow. Since Lean is focused on defining value for the customer and eliminating waste, why wouldn't everyone want to do it? The reason may be that much of our behavior, at *all* staff levels, is governed by our beliefs about how things work. Many of the improvement strategies of Lean and continuous improvement often do not make sense under existing behaviors and beliefs. *BTC's* challenge was not just the application of techniques; it was developing an entirely new way of thinking and looking at work. Not surprisingly, then, it took time and effort for it to be reflected in the culture.

BTC demonstrated that Lean principles and methods work in government, that they can be enthusiastically embraced by employees, and that they offer a unique opportunity to transform government and its beliefs about itself. *BTC* supported state employees as catalysts for this change. This move toward a changing culture was increasingly evidenced by:

- **A move to a shared Lean language**. A shared language is key to culture. Government staff were beginning to use this language and apply what it means—that government does have processes, does have customers, does have products, and does affect outcomes for its customers—in their daily work. Staff understood what *waste* is, what *value-added* means, and that a problem is an opportunity for improvement.

- **A slowly growing understanding that improving one's work is part of the work and incorporating Lean in their daily work.** This was reflected in increased participation in continuous improvement events/projects, participation in the DOPs, and validation by the attention/requests from outside the state of Maine. As one state employee explained, they incorporated "Integration of LEAN principles into our day-to-day work, decision-making, analysis. Now, many of us automatically identify waste or redundant/unnecessary activity. As a matter of course, some of us are beginning to work these concepts into our creation of new processes so that we start out more efficiently than we may have before."
- **Increased acceptance of Lean continuous improvement as a legitimate and deliberate way of making improvements.** As shown by an increased number of requests to *BTC* to facilitate improvement work.
- **Use of a disciplined problem-solving approach and development of a process mindset.** Staff understanding that problems are the result of processes, not people. Understanding what a process was and how they participated in the flow of worked almost always proved to be a significant insight for staff. We often saw relationships change throughout a three-day improvement event as staff actually could see where problems were in their work.
- **Increased use of, demand for, and reliance on qualitative and quantitative data in planning and making decisions.** Making changes based on facts/data rather than emotion. Value stream mapping proved to be a powerful tool for managers to see and understand the problems and waste that exist in their respective processes. This also proved to be a significant driver to make changes.
- **A legitimization of the expectation that the people doing the work, providing the services, and using government's services and products must be part of planning and decision-making.** Managers increased willingness to commit staff and teams to do the improvement work. It was always the case that at the beginning of an improvement event, CIPs could guarantee that improvement would be found in their work. This, of course,

was because it was the actual people doing the work that knew about the problems and suggested how to improve them.

Important Observed Outcomes

- **Increased awareness of Lean principles and methods in the government and service sectors.** This was evidenced by:
    - o The numbers of CIPs (seventy-eight trained) and *BTC* participants (over one thousand)
    - o Multistate collaboration and recognition
    - o Use of our materials by external entities
    - o An emerging shared Lean language
    - o Expressed interest by Maine's gubernatorial candidates
    - o Engagement with other public sector entities, such as the University of Maine
    - o The level of participation in the August Lean Systems Summit.
- **Conversion of manufacturing methods and tools to government sector.** *BTC* developed standardized tool kits for its CIPs. These tool kits were modified/customized from manufacturing models to meet government/service sector environments. This customization was based on feedback from working with state employees and their ability to understand a language that at times seemed foreign to them.

Savings/Gains/Benefits Realized.

Much of the work of *BTC* was reflected in the results of the improvements made by *BTC* and the programs and agencies. Selected examples are included below.

Improvement Initiatives:

- Using common conventions and standards enabled improvement project results to be compared between improvement initiative summaries and reports. An example is the use of a standard convention to convert state staff time saved to money—the fully burdened cost—last computed at an average of fifty-eight cents per minute.
- Resulted in the use of 12 percent attrition as opposed to layoffs, reflecting a longer-range view. For example, MDOL has been the only labor department that did not lay off staff during this period.
- *BTC* documented an overall savings of $16 million for agencies participating in improvement initiatives.

Improvement Project Teams: Over seventy improvement interventions, not counting educational/training sessions, were conducted. Selected recent examples appear below:

- **Employment Posting**. By eliminating steps and simplifying the intake form for employer requests to listing new jobs, businesses could post job openings directly to the Maine career center job bank twenty-four hours a day over the internet.
- **For customers with disabilities seeking employment/retraining services**, the wait list was twelve months before a project team reorganized the application and entry process. This led to a complete elimination of the waiting list, even as demand for services grew during the recession. It has also allowed the program to lower the qualification threshold for services, allowing even more people to benefit from the program.
- **Adoptions**. The goal was to improve the timeliness to adoption for children in foster care with a termination of parental rights, increasing the number of foster children in permanent homes. In 2005 only 11 percent of the total foster care populations were adopted; in 2009 this was more than doubled to 23 percent.
- **HETL/Environmental Inorganics Lab**. Improvements included the reduction in sample turnaround time from an average of nine days in 2006 to five days in 2010 and four days in 2009, allowing the section to function with one less FTE and one less seasonal employee in the section and a monetary savings in excess of $60,000 annually. Potential savings, if recommended improvements were fully implemented, was estimated at $102,973.
- **Autism/Pervasive Developmental Disabilities (PDD) System**. Focused on two prioritized areas: early identification and transition to adulthood. Following the success of four screening pilots in 2009, MaineCare added the new screening protocol to their well-child visit forms. As well, the PDD initiative and Maine CDC sponsored trainings for physicians on adding the new screening protocol and why the new screening is important.

BTC was initially worked with state employees and state processes and structures. These were the people and processes that provided and delivered service to Maine citizens. We felt as these improved, of necessity services to Maine citizens would improve as well. During *BTC's* operation, Maine state government comprised about ten thousand employees statewide, including leadership, managers, and all other members of the workforce. *BTC* worked directly with about 10 percent of the state workforce. *BTC* started with the departments and agencies within the executive branch and intended to collaborate actively with the other two government branches (judiciary and legislative), as well as with government's partners in the private sector.

Working from Pull: As noted above, *BTC* became involved in improvement efforts at the request of program/process leaders/managers, although anyone could bring a problem or need to its attention. The number of individuals actively involved at any given point varied considerably based on the improvement projects underway, awareness trainings being offered, workshops being conducted, and ongoing follow-up/mentoring with individuals and teams that had been implementing improvements. The size of improvement teams typically ranged from six to twenty-nine individuals with an average of around twelve.

Improvement projects included government's clients/customers, suppliers, and partners/providers as part of improvement teams. Not surprisingly, this was desirable and fruitful, and the departments consistently supported this broad-based involvement. Specific examples included clients, family members, and providers on the pervasive developmental disorders service system design team and the long-term care in-home and community-based services system team and employers (customers) on the governor's training initiative VSM and rapid improvement teams.

Barriers encountered: As we reflected on the work *BTC* did over this period, we were faced with a variety of obstacles. Some of these became particularly acute as *BTC* evolved. The following lists the challenges that emerged and the strategies we used to overcome them.

Leadership and Management: While the initial leadership for MDOL and DHHS was committed to transforming government work culture, they did not have the overt commitment of the governor's office or the legislature. As a result, the long-range vision and commitment needed to drive Lean and continuous improvement throughout all state departments was lacking. The type of transformation envisioned by *BTC* leaders takes time and constancy of purpose. It requires long-range commitment to build an improvement ethos and corresponding infrastructure. This can be difficult in government where key players can change every election year. *BTC* sought to build a structure that would transcend the constant turnover of elected officials.

Unlearning of Twentieth Century and Older Management Practices: These processes were being taught in most MBA/MPA programs. By moving from an authoritarian and blame/shame approach to a problem-solving one proved difficult. Something as simple as focused, concentrated improvement sessions is not generally the way business is conducted in government. Strings of meetings are more typically the norm, so what could be done by Lean in a short time might take months to do, if at all.

BTC addressed this in its collaboration with the University of Maine system to incorporate Lean into its leadership and business curricula. Similarly, *BTC* worked with the state human resources (five CIPs were HR staff) Maine management service to focus on incoming staff on the "new" way of doing business in government.

Focusing on Process Improvement Rather Than on a Changing Mindset: This obstacle was, in a way, progress for it reflected that government was recognizing that it has processes and that they can be improved. However, the challenge was for *BTC* to infuse a problem-solving *mindset* in all staff and how they view and do their work—as part of both a personal paradigm and organizational culture.

A Graying Workforce/Succession Management: Many leaders in *BTC* and in the workforce were retiring or close to retirement, and there was concern about how to sustain this effort into a subsequent administration and beyond. *BTC* worked with business leaders to ensure that the current and new government leaders understood the value of the *BTC* initiative in these difficult fiscally challenging times. This was the primary purpose of developing the Lean summit to provide an opportunity for business leaders to come together with government employees to build support in the wider business community.

Dedicated *BTC* Time for CIPs: Although CIPs and their supervisors made a commitment to active *BTC* participation, as "volunteers" CIPs faced significant challenges in finding and managing the time for *BTC* improvement and ongoing self-development activities. Given increasing demand, this had a significant impact on the capacity and work of *BTC*.

BTC developed a template language to be included in their annual performance evaluations so that *BTC* participation would be planned, expected, and supported as part of their work.

Fear and Uncertainty: Juran would call this "cultural resistance." Some staff, at all levels, would say that Lean improvement work was interrupting their real work; was unnecessary because things work OK and they don't have any "waste;" because they already know what the problem is and how to solve it, was putting them in jeopardy of losing their job; was telling them what to do; was taking time they don't have; or was not going to work because it won't be implemented. Although these objections diminished as team members participated in improvement intervention(s), the challenge for *BTC* was spreading staff awareness and acceptance that improving the work *is* the work and produces significant savings and benefits to them and their customers.

Lessons Learned

Executive Leadership: Executive leadership in Maine state government consists of the governor and his immediate cabinet, which consists of departmental commissioners. *BTC* was fortunate to have the commissioners of two significant state departments, the Department of Labor and the Department of Health and Human Services, support its activities. Despite this, *BTC* was unable to get the full attention of the governor's office. However, *BTC* did support and do improvement work in other state departments. In addition to MDOL and DHHS, *BTC* recruited CIPs from the departments of Financial and Administrative Affairs, Transportation, Corrections, and Environmental Protection. These CIPs did improvement work in their respective departments and also participated as members of CIP improvement teams assisting other departments in VSM and kaizen work. They also attended clinical sessions and other *BTC* trainings. What did not happen was a recognition from the governor's office that the capability to make process improvements across all state departments would have a huge strategic value in transforming state government. We knew that leaders' and managers' beliefs, constancy, and commitment to improvement were essential to the effectiveness of any transformation. Yet *BTC* was not able to engage executive leadership in aligning departments' strategic priorities to *BTC* initiatives. Therefore, this did not optimize *BTC* capabilities and influence. Ideally, Lean thinking would have cascaded down from the governor's throughout all state departments as an operational excellence tool. *BTC* needed to be presented in a more strategic and disciplined manner, for executives to understand the Lean message and to support them in actively instilling and modeling Lean principles throughout their programs.

Prioritizing Improvements: State employees think of work as being their "regular" work (both work done well and not so well) while improvement work was something extra to do. Given the current culture and structure, leaders and managers typically did not prioritize improvement in their daily work. They would point out that they did not have time, even though they spent time, sometimes lots of it, dealing with crises, errors, and rework. Many struggled with the idea that improving the work and eliminating the rework would yield more time. They also struggled with putting into practice expressed beliefs of valuing the people doing the work by, for example, giving them the authority to make improvements in their work, be creative, and take reasonable risks. In addition, significantly, many managers did not have the project management knowledge or skills needed in order to implement improvement projects.

Marketing Success: *BTC* was remarkably successful from the onset of doing improvement work.

At one of our first-year improvement events, a rookie CIP team mapped a value stream for the delivery of death records to the public, reducing the delivery time from ninety to five days. This became national news and was reported in the *Chicago Tribune*! As a result of this rapid turnaround, we had a person from California call and praise the vital records team for getting his relative's death records in such a short period of time, saying to the receptionist, "I am going to move to Maine to die"! As it turned out, many of the improvements had significant success in identifying and improving work. It became a standard belief that we could guarantee improvements to teams that we worked with. We worked to improve services to citizens by improving delivery times, simplifying, and standardizing work, and documenting cost savings. What *BTC* failed to capitalize on was the marketing of these successes, particularly to executive management. Had we done a better job of this, we might have been able to capture their attention more effectively. *BTC* was also unable to get legislative attention to the work we were doing. Presentations were made to some legislative committees, but unlike other states which did get legislation passed requiring state departments to have a Lean program, and although we sought to have this occur in Maine, we were unable to make this happen. We believe in part this was because the gains we saw in the field were not adequately translated to the executive and legislative arenas. Additional lessons are listed in the table below and are displayed in three categories, namely (1) getting started, (2) implementation, and (3) sustaining.

Getting Started Lessons

Develop executive and senior leadership support	This is the most important lesson learned from *BTC*. Although *BTC* initially had commissioner-level support, we never had the chance to provide a thorough understanding of value and benefits of Lean/ continuous improvement principles and methods to executive-level management.
Integrate Lean/CI into strategic planning	In our TQM experience, the governor chaired a quality council; while at the time this was not a Lean initiative, it did make TQM and executive leadership visible and a focus for all of state government. This did not happen with *BTC*, and therefore a huge opportunity in productivity and cost reductions was lost.
Engage and involve middle management	*BTC* did involve middle management in many of its improvement events, but because Lean/CI was not seen as a strategic goal for all of government, their involvement was not consistent nor coordinated with strategic goals.
Get expert help	Since Lean is often described as being counterintuitive (i.e., doing more with less), it is critically important to have experts with significant experience for those first exposed to it. In some ways, its early adoption must be faith based (i.e., that it can and will work here).
Secure a budget line	*BTC* would not have had a chance to develop had not commissioners provided start-up funding as well as secured a budget line to support its activities. A small investment here proved to have significant ROI for overall state operations.
Commit FTEs	There needs to be someone leading a Lean start-up. This is particularly the case for large organizations. At DHHS we were fortunate to have 2.5 FTEs assigned for the Lean start-up, and this turned out to work for a department of approximately 3,800 staff.
Track your ROI	From the start *BTC* recognized the importance of documenting results. MDOL developed an Excel tool that enabled CIPs to quantify gains from improvement events and convert them into dollar savings. This enabled *BTC* to quantify and track gains. Unfortunately, this tool was not consistently applied for every improvement event; thus we were not able to show ROI in all improvement events.

Implementation Lessons

Work from pull not push	Pull is an important concept in Lean, and we applied it to implementing improvements. We did not attempt to force Lean on to managers but sought to market it to them through awareness sessions and worked only with those managers who invited us to "try it out" on problems they were having in the respective departments. Once early successes were achieved, these served as a powerful marketing tool for more invitations to do work
Develop standardized materials	*BTC* developed design notes for every improvement activity. This was considered standard practice for every event and enabled CIPs to think through and document how they were going to work with an improvement team. These were continuously improved upon and customized for every event and provided a standardized guide for CIPS to follow in their work with improvement teams.
Just do it	It was not unusual for CIPs to feel intimidated leading an improvement team for the first time even after forty hours of a DOP session. The real learning is in the practice of using the tools and methods of Lean. Having standardized tools, design notes, and participant workbooks not only provided guides but also confidence for CIPs to successfully facilitate improvement teams.
Find a dedicated space	Ideally, all work should be done in the workplace or *gemba*. Unfortunately, government operations and space requirements were not conducive to working with large teams. We found out early on that there was a lot of transportation waste in moving CIPs and people to find adequate space to do mapping work, for example. Developing *BTC's* Lean Lab was a huge innovation, and it was used consistently for all training and improvement events, saving considerable time and excess people movement.

Implementation Lessons (continued)

Plan for improvements up front	One of the first items to discuss with sponsors seeking to do an improvement event is how do they plan to do the improvements that are identified by the improvement team. We often found that once an improvement action plan was developed by a team, there was often stress on the team as to who would do the work and how improvement would actually be completed.
Develop the concept of buffer resources	It was sometimes the case that improvement team members could not attend improvement events because there was no one to do their work when they were attending an improvement event. Buffer resources are resources that can be temporarily relied upon to fill in when a staff resource is not available. This is not a concept that state workers are familiar with but one that can be extremely useful in improvement work.
Be prepared for mentoring/ coaching	Since Lean principles and methods were unfamiliar to state workers, efforts in coaching and mentoring are important in achieving success. We found this to be particularly true for developing and training CIPs, hence the development of a certification process that required newly trained CIPs to be mentored by certified CIPs.

Sustaining Lessons

Focus on developing a process mindset	We found most state employees at all levels did not have a clear understanding of a process despite many saying that they did. It was almost always the case that the mapping process was revelatory for staff. We were always amazed about the impact this had on how employees rethought about their work.
Be aware of "hard" and "soft" outcomes	Not only were we interested in having staff understand and apply Lean/CI concepts (the hard aspect) but we also saw changes in the relational dynamics of the process improvement team (the soft aspect). Staff began to see their work was dependent on others in the process and the consequences when it was not done well or delayed. We saw this reflection of relation coordination, a concept developed by Jody Hoffer Gittell and an important outcome of improvement work.
Develop private and public partnerships	*BTC* realized that since Lean was an unknown concept, particularly in the state workforce, it was important to reach out to other organizations using Lean. This was one purpose of the *BTC* study missions, to not only learn about what these organizations were doing but also to let them know what we were doing. This was also one reason we developed the Lean summit to invite private and public organizations to see, hear and share the work being done using Lean to improve their organizations.
Market and celebrate success	Marketing success is critical to keep a Lean initiative going, especially in the early stages of implementation. Once successes are seen, Lean will "sell" itself. This is one reason we were able to keep *BTC* going despite not having executive-level success.
Don't forget constancy of purpose	Deming's number one point for management. There will be many barriers and setbacks in any new initiative, particularly in the early stages of a start-up. Stay focused and don't give up. Setbacks and barriers are just another set of problems to be solved.

Best efforts will not substitute for knowledge.
—W. Edwards Deming

EPILOGUE

The ability to successfully adapt a manufacturing model to government processes and functions speaks to the flexibility and replicability of this program to other government structures and environments. A key feature was the development of the *BTC* structure and internal capacity. We saw these elements as innovative. We believe that Bend the Curve is applicable to a variety of governmental settings and service sectors.

This is evidenced by other entities acknowledging the materials *BTC* developed. Some sought us out directly for consultation and instruction. *BTC* produced a wide array of government-oriented processes, methodologies, and materials that were available and used by other external entities. At the time, these were posted on our website and included the following:

- Innovative and detailed training and facilitation design note formats
- Introductory and advanced week-long trainings (using an adult learning model of learning by doing) on Lean principles and methods, team building, and self/organizational development skills
- A variety other training activities and simulations
- A traditional and new integrated version of value stream mappings
- Customized rapid improvement events/kaizens
- Monthly team clinical supervision (the typical standardized agenda format, developed by the CIPs, includes learning modules, research/reading discussions, intervention updates, Lean methodology and tool practice,

and a hands-on "lab" segment; this is seen as critical to ongoing CIP development)

- Hands-on activities/exercises that illustrate Lean concepts
- A "job" description for a CIP, outlining the responsibilities and qualities for the role
- A CIP certification process
- Protocols for structured observation, study missions, and CIP selection.
- A CIP assessment based on five competencies (self, group, change, Lean, process)
- An exam for certification

Many of the process improvements accomplished through *BTC* were cross-functional within programs/departments and/or cut across program and department silos. Examples include access for state employees to information resources and integrated client eligibility and access to services.

Service New Brunswick; the Town of Durham, New Hampshire; and New Hampshire DHHS have visited Maine's Bend the Curve program and website and incorporated aspects of *BTC* in their own work, adapting it and its materials to meet their specific needs. Durham sent four town officials to the *BTC* week-long introductory training. Both they and NH DHHS have continued their involvement with *BTC* and are part of the Continuous Improvement Lean Collaborative, initiated by *BTC*, which plans and conducts the annual Lean Systems Summit from 2012 to the present. The collaborative meets regularly by teleconferencing.

BTC's name reflects its intent to improve government services and quality as resources diminish (i.e., do more, better, and at less cost) by the following:

a. **Internal, Embedded Training and Practice Capacity**: Rather than relying on external consultants, *BTC* sought to train an internal "volunteer" interdepartmental team of continuous improvement practitioners (CIPs) in Lean and other process/system improvement principles and methods. These CIPs held a variety of positions at various levels in their agencies. *BTC* work was incorporated as a part of their ongoing work. With the support of their supervisors, they lead and mentored process improvement activities in their respective agencies and throughout state government. The intent was to seed and grow Lean throughout state government and its partners.
b. **Transformation of a Manufacturing Model into One for Government**: Translating Lean methodology and tools to a government environment

required considerable time and effort based on *BTC's* growing experience and learning. *BTC* developed a variety of templates, processes, tools, design notes, reference guide, and other materials for use in government and other service/transaction sectors.

c. **Continuous Development**: *BTC's* structure provided for intensive and ongoing trainings, workshops, monthly clinicals, and study missions. A clear standardized certification process was developed for staff who wanted to become CIPs.

Support: In addition to the commissioners and deputy commissioners, the strongest supporters of the Lean philosophy and the Bend the Curve program, not surprisingly, have generally been the individuals who've participated directly in an improvement or design team, understood its significance/likely benefit, and experienced "success." There were others who, apart from any experience, were excited by the ideas and possibilities in the Lean concepts themselves and their application to government. In addition, and unexpectedly, the other strongest supporters have been external entities with whom Bend the Curve has worked and/or consulted, such as the New Hampshire Department of Health and Human Services, the University of Southern Maine's Muskie Center for Public Service and Lewiston-Auburn College, and the Town of Durham, New Hampshire.

A Note about Barriers: Some members of management felt there was not enough time for this work and that they could not support staff "taking time off" to do it; some also had fear of giving up control to workers or cited the staff and financial cost without considering the return on investment. There were also staff who blamed *BTC* rather than their program for a failure to implement recommended improvements, as well as those who had a strong "here we go again" reaction. The most vociferous critics tended to be those who feared the effect of a change on them and their work or those who would have to change their way of doing things as a result of an improvement change, particularly when it resulted in the elimination of work that the individuals were responsible for. However, as the DHHS vital records improvement project manager noted, "Any kind of change is always difficult for staff. With the value stream mapping process, however, staff becomes an owner of the mapping of tasks and sees the benefits in the reduction in time, resources, and steps necessary to accomplish a goal."

A Final Note: Lean is a business strategy. It is one of the most effective ever developed, being designed to deliver the highest value to customers at the lowest possible cost and used throughout the world with success. Every business and government administration faces the challenges of managing order and chaos that exist in the workplace. Order means we get what we expect while chaos means we do not. Work always seems to fluctuate between the two. Lean thinking is an organizational strategy designed to manage the dynamic that exists between order and chaos in every organization. It is often the case that an elected official will make the case that they intended to manage government as a business with the intention to improve government and deliver better and more cost-effective services than their predecessor. We believe this is the right sentiment, but the question of *how* to do it is rarely effectively addressed. We heard this sentiment many times during our tenure as civil servants. Yet despite these proclamations, few saw Lean thinking as a solution; more often than not, few even knew much about Lean and, sadly, didn't seem to care all that much to know or learn, which begs the question: Why not? We believe in part the answer lies in Lean not being part of their business and educational experience. It is also partly the hubris of executives thinking they already know the what and the how of managing complex systems—after all, they got elected or promoted! As widely used as Lean is throughout organizations around the world, it is a constant surprise to us how few people know about Lean as a successful management strategy. This is one reason why we at *BTC* first created an annual Lean Summit to provide a forum to further disseminate these ideas. *BTC* in Maine state government no longer exists. We view our work with *BTC* as a grand experiment in state government where new ideas were tried and tested and given the effort and leadership by many, an unqualified success, yet here we are at the end. When TQM died in Maine, it gave rise, phoenix like, to a new idea,: Lean, in the form of *BTC*. We hope with this book and the seeds that were sown by *BTC* and the human spirit to continuously improve, something new will rise again.

CHRONOLOGICAL TIME FRAME FOR *BTC*

State Fiscal Year (SFY) July 1 to June 30, 2004–05: This was the launching of the Bend the Curve program and its evolution into a state of Maine initiative, with many of the "firsts":

- DHHS began weekly Lean discussions/implementation with leadership/staff: Summer 2004.
- MDOL department-wide and leadership trainings conducted: summer/fall 2004.
- DHHS began first training/mentoring and improvement projects: summer/fall 2004.
- MDOL two pilot VSMs conducted: 9–10/04.
- MDOL Lean "Wave" (blitz of eighteen concurrent VSMs on one day): 11/04.
- First two week-long introductory development of practitioners (DOP) trainings held: DOP1-1 January 2005 and DOP1-2 June 2005.
- First monthly full-day clinical supervision held: 2/05.
- MDOL Bend the Curve "fairs": throughout 2005.

SFY 2005–06: Two major advances stand out—the development and provision of an advanced five-day Lean training practicum and the creation of the DHHS Office of Lean Management.

- Advanced week-long DOP2-1 training conducted: 10/05
- DHHS Office of Lean Management (OLM) established: 1/06
- Study mission process and protocol standardized and expanded: 6/06
- Improvement interventions conducted and observed: throughout SFY

- DOP1-3 held: 5/06
- First CIP certified: 5/06

SFY 2006–07: Three major innovations were implemented—the development of supporting structures for CIPs, a certification process, and CIP assumption of clinical planning and facilitation.

- *BTC* website and *CIP News* newsletter launched: summer 2006
- Lean "Managing in State Government" course delivered: 10/06
- CIP certification kaizen conducted: 11/06
- Clinical supervision planning and facilitation assumed by CIPs: 4/07
- First internal study mission (to MeCDC HETL): 5/07

SFY 2007–2008: State CIPs, without external consultants, conducted the week-long and other trainings and performed Lean interventions—a major goal in line with *BTC*'s internal development strategy.

- DOP 1-4 held: 9/07
- Presentation to Legislative OPEGA oversight committee: summer 2007
- Planning of public: private "Maine Lean Summit" began: winter 2007–08
- Collaboration with the state training unit began: 5/08
- Collaboration and regular teleconferencing with other states exploring/implementing Lean: spring 2008
- External consultant contracts ended: summer 2008

SFY 2008–2009: Moved toward integrating other continuous improvement approaches into its more "traditional" Lean approach.

- Ken Miller workshops held: 12/08 and 3–4/09
- OLM moved to headquarters building and established Lean Learning Lab: 11/08
- "Practicum in Lean Management" training conducted: 11/08

SFY 2009–2010: Intensified collaboration with entities outside state of Maine government, not only to exchange knowledge and experiences and further the development of Lean leaders and managers coming into the state but also to create a Lean groundswell.

- Active strategy and curriculum development with DAFS-BHR: monthly throughout the year

- Collaboration with the University of Southern Maine/Lewiston-Auburn College began: fall 2009.
- Study mission from Town of Durham, New Hampshire, conducted: 8/09
- Study mission from NH DHHS conducted: 10/09
- DOP 1-5 conducted: 3/10

SFY 2010–11: Focused on strategies for enhancing Lean implementation within government and its partners.

- Strategy drafted to prepare for change in administrations: spring/summer 2010
- Lean Systems Summit—Northeast held in Portland, Maine: 8/13/10
- Recipient of the Bright Ideas award from Harvard University's Ash Center for Democratic Governance and Innovation at the John F. Kennedy School of Business

SFY 2011–12: As directed, *BTC* ceased operations, and the website was taken down and moved to a nonstate site. The offspring Continuous Improvement Lean Collaborative continues, holding its annual Lean Systems Summit.

ACKNOWLEDGMENTS

First and foremost, we would like to acknowledge Laura Fortman and Jack Nicholas, commissioners of the Department of Labor (MDOL) and the Department of Health and Human Service, respectively, for having the insight and courage to provide the initial resources and ongoing support for *BTC*.

To a very large extent, were it not for Commissioner Laura Fortman's and Deputy Commissioner Jane Gilbert's support for both their financial acumen and wisdom in seeing that MDOL could be been successful in fundamentally improving how it operated and take a chance to break with tradition and try something unique for state government. They also made a point of making *BTC* available to all comers. Thanks also to our consultants, Dr. Susan M. Gallant, Janet Eastman, and Jon Kirsch; *BTC* would not be *BTC* without their tireless efforts, knowledge, and broadness of thought. Especially important were their knowledge of systems and systems thinking, their knowledge of processing and their ability to process in ways which proved to be invaluable, and Susan's ability and willingness to call things as she saw them. Janet Eastman, as a talented consultant and trainer, provided ongoing support for this effort. They helped us understand the importance of group facilitation and team building and the challenging issues we would face around sustaining organizational change. Jon Kirsch brought many years of private sector Lean implementation and training and proved to be our astute "technical" Lean production consultant and was right at home in a government environment. He applied Lean in an environment where others said it wouldn't work.

Special thanks to *BTC*'s immediate staff, Lita Klavins, Rae Ann Brann and John Rioux, for their willingness to participate as staff in what was a novel idea and their support of the vision, values, and mission of *BTC*. The authors would have made little progress without their insights, hard work, and support. Lita Klavins gave up an IT position to fully commit her time to bringing Lean systems thinking to state government. Lita became a go-to person for all things related to the work of continuous improvement practitioners. Her work in editing a draft of this book was invaluable, and without her support this book would not have been possible. John Rioux, a highly respected statistician, reminded us that "if you don't measure it, you haven't changed it." And "if haven't measurably reduced time thus costs, again your investment in dollars and time and not worth it." John measured. His measurements were known to be accurate, factual, and trusted, and we relied on him. John also developed an Excel spreadsheet that we used to track and quantify process improvements. His review and comments on this manuscript were also very much appreciated. Lita and John continue to this day providing leadership at the annual Lean Summit held in Portland, Maine, every summer and represent a continuing legacy of Bend the Curve. Additional thanks to Kimberly Smith for her financial acumen in keeping *BTC* "on the rails" and Merle Davis for embracing Lean thinking and selflessly contributing to event planning and facilitation and for serving as one of *BTC*'s expert trainers. Thanks also to Nancy DeSisto, who made the important link from her classroom experience to her commissioner's attention and hence made the launch of *BTC* at DHHS. And a very special thanks to all the Continuous Improvement Practitioners (CIPS) who worked with us over the eight years of *BTC*'s existence; their willingness to learn something new, their dedication to improving government operations, and sharing their unique knowledge and skills to their staff and teams they worked with. Finally, a special thanks to those government managers who saw Lean as a new powerful and productive way to make positive change happen and were unafraid to try it out in their respective departments.

ABOUT THE AUTHORS

Dr. Walter E. Lowell

Dr. Lowell was the former director of the Office of Lean Management for the Maine Department of Health and Human Services and was also a leader in the state of Maine's collaborative, interdepartmental continuous improvement *BTC* program. His responsibilities included the design and implementation of the Office of Lean Management for the Department of Health and Human Services reporting to the office of the commissioner. The work included managing the office; strategic planning; organizational development; process improvement; working with staff at all levels of the organization; training and leading teams in Lean systems knowledge and methods, including value stream mapping and kaizen events; and coordinating with other state agencies on Lean practices with savings in excess of $4 million dollars. As a leader of the Bend the Curve program, Dr. Lowell was the founder of Maine's annual Lean summit, held each summer in Portland, Maine. Dr. Lowell also teaches university level courses and consults on Lean and continuous improvement.

Arthur Davis

Arthur served as director of operations, Maine Department of Labor/*BTC* Program Coordinator (*BTC*, also known as "Operational Excellence"), imitated the program. He studied the Toyota Production System in Japan and initiated, planned, and managed the transformation to "Lean" in two US manufacturing plants. He formally studied Six Sigma and TQC in the United States and Japan. While implementing his first Lean transformation, he studied and learned from Dr. Ichiro Miyauchi, senior total quality consultant, Union of Japanese Scientists and Engineers.

The Department of Labor rolled out Lean in June 2004 to all 630 (then) of its employees. Commissioner Laura Fortman appointed Arthur to Labor, with approval of Governor John E. Baldacci, in part to help the department fundamentally change how work is done.

GLOSSARY OF ABBREVIATIONS

BHR	Bureau of Human Resources
BTC	Bend the Curve
CDC	Center for Disease Control
CI	Continuous Improvement
COT	Cost of time
CS	Current state
DAFS	Department of Administrative Affairs
DEC	Digital Equipment Corporation
DHHS	Department of Health and Human Services
DN	Design notes
DOP	Development of practitioners
FS	Future state
FTE	Full-time equivalent
HETL	Health and Environmental Testing Laboratory
IAP	Improvement action plan
LTC	Long-term care
MDOL	Maine Department of Labor
NVA	Nonvalue added
OCS	Office of Children's Services
OIAS	Office of Integrated Access and Support
OIT	Office of Information Technology
OLMS	Office of Labor-Management Standards
OPEGA	Office of Program Evaluation and Government Accountability
PDD	Primary Developmental Disorder
PPT	PowerPoint
PW	Participant workbook
RC	Relational coordination
TPS	Toyota Production System
TQM	Total quality management
VA	Value added
VSM	Value stream map

APPENDICES

APPENDIX A

DHHS Selected Work

Process	DHHS Department	*Projected Annual Savings
Waiver Funding	OACPD	$73,476.00
IR Access	DHHS-DAFS/OIT	$318,841.00
In-State Travel	DHHS	$7,395.00
Complaint Investigations	Licensing	$96,523.00
Microbiology	HETL	$120,582.00
Adoption Services	OCS	$1,057,999.00
Child Day Care	OCS	$700,000.00
Revenue Deposit	DAFS	$14,616.00
Totals	*DHHS*	$2,389,432.00

* Does not include other saving and related benefits

DHHS Projected Savings Example

Average saving per process:

$298,679.00

If we worked on 20 process/year

$298, 679.00 X 20 processes =

$5,973,580.00 per year

Savings accrued after 4 years

X 4 years =

$23,894,320.00

Projected Cost Savings with Lean Implementation for State Budget*

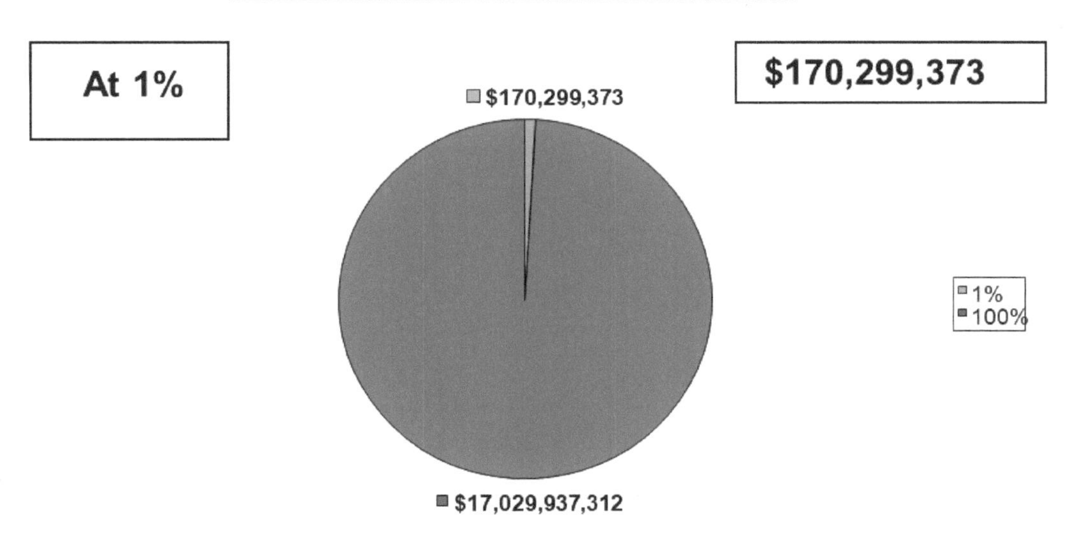

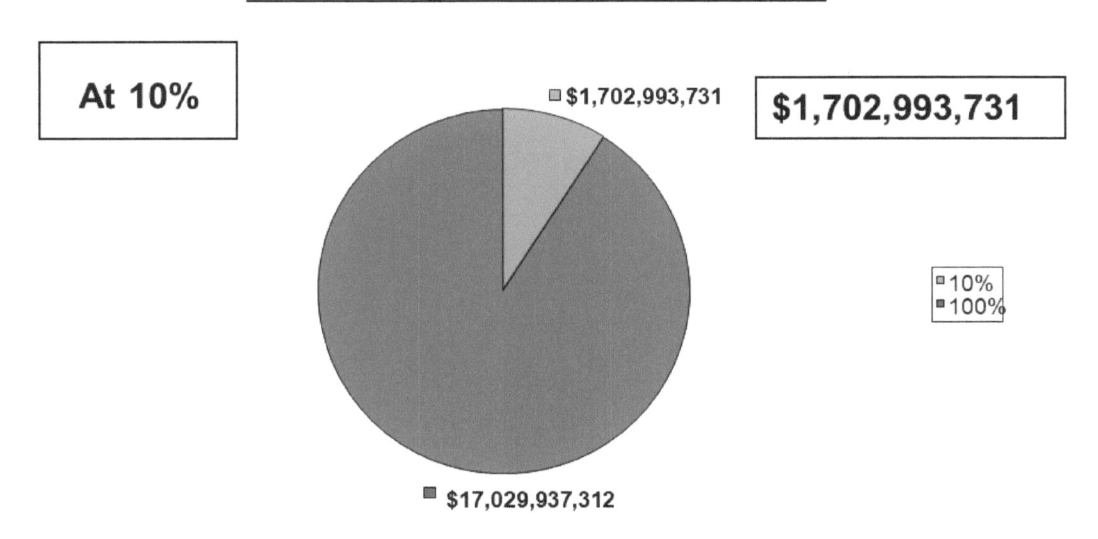

APPENDIX B

Design Notes: VSM—Day Two Future State

P = Participant; HO = Handout; FC = Flip chart; PW = Participant workbook

TABLE OF CONTENTS

Appendices:

- Questions for Analyzing the Current State of Your Process in Order to Make Improvements*
- Questions to Consider in Developing the Improvement Action Plan

Design Notes: VSM Day Two—Future State

7:30–8:15 **Set Up and Prep for VSM**
- Clean and set up room
- Practitioner team "huddle"—review roles and development goals

8:15–8:30 **Start Up in VSM Teams**
- Introductions as needed
- Logistics and overview of day and summary of work done.
- Check in

8:30–10:00 **Complete Current State Steps' Elapsed and Work Times**
- Identify elapsed and work times (HO)
- Summarize CS times
- Review data and discuss the three Bs: batch, backlog, bottleneck (PW p. 43)

10:00–10:15 ***Break*** (remind to order lunch)
- Meet with CI practitioner team

10:15–11:00 **Identifying Wastes, Applying Lean Concepts and Analysis**
- Worksheet: identifying eight wastes (PW p. 41), applying Lean concepts (PW pp. 44–47), and analysis questions (PW pp. 53–54)
- Conduct VA and NVA activity (PW p. 39)
- Review/analyze and discuss again CS elapsed and work times
- Assess overall flow

11:00–12:00 **Prepare for Future State Mapping**
- BO: Divide Ps into three small groups.
- Ask them to discuss and answer process analysis questions (PW pp. 53–54—Miller HO)
- Whole Team: Discuss results and record, as appropriate, on poster.

12:00–12:30 ***Lunch***
- Meet with CI practitioner team
- Assess where team is and make adjustments as needed

12:30–1:30 **Begin Future State Mapping**

- Review charter and matrix as needed
- Worksheet: future state mapping (PW p. 60)
  - BO: Ask each group to begin creating a future state using Post-its

1:30–2:15 **Continue Future State Mapping**

- Using BO groups' Post-its, begin building FS using green step sheets.
- Identify any potential kaizens (red bursts)

2:15–2:30 ***Break***

- Meet with CI practitioner team
- Set Up for improvement action plan (if indicated)

2:30–3:45 **Finish Future State Mapping**

- Complete mapping of FS in whole team, identifying WT and ET times

3:45–4:15 **Calculate Future State Times**

- Calculate FS summary time data.
- Compare and analyze CS and FS times.

4:15–4:30 **Wrap Up**

- Summarize action items and next steps
- Check Out
- Appreciation

Time/Topic	Purpose and Method	Materials Resources
7:30–8:15 Set up and Prep for VSM	**Purpose:** · Participants experience a well-organized, confidant, competent, and professional learning experience—all in service to enabling the team to accomplish their task and have a satisfying experience. **Methodology:** · Be sure room is clean, debris removed, and all materials and equipment organized for the day. · Meet with VSM staff/CIPs and review roles, responsibilities, and any development goals. · Review the current state calculations (metrics spreadsheet) to assess if there is a need to highlight anything specific today.	· HOs, PW Workbook
8:15–8:30 Start Up in VSM Teams	**Purpose:** · Clarify expectations and create a shared understanding of the direction for the day. · Continue developing as a team · Reconnect with each other and the work of day one **Methodology:** · Make any introductions that are needed (staff, observers, new participants) · Review safety exits · Review logistics (restrooms, breaks, lunch) · Review day one · Preview today's agenda and outcomes	

Time/Topic	Purpose and Method	Materials Resources
	· Check in: One word or sentence (not a paragraph) about how you are doing as we start the day today (idea, feeling, observation, et cetera); from whoever starts, we will go round-robin to the left until we have everyone checked in · Make note of any themes or patterns you noted during the check-in that could impact the work today	
8:30–10:00 COMPLETE CURRENT STATE STEPS AND TIME DATA METRICS	**Purpose:** · Finish a shared visualization of the LTC current state · Identify and practice using elapsed and work times · Reinforce the usefulness of collecting the data. **Methodology:** · Review the work done to date on the current state steps. o If time allows and if appropriate, ask if any steps are missing (refer to the maps done in the three groups) and what steps are needed to complete the process. o Adjust the existing CS map accordingly. · When the entire process has been completed, return to the first step and explain that the team will now begin to identify the time it takes to accomplish each step. · Refer Ps to the step sheet (PW p. 36). · Remind Ps of the meaning and significance of elapsed time and work time. · Identify the elapsed time and work time for each step.	· Step Sheet—PW p. 36 · 3Bs—PW p. 43

Time/Topic	Purpose and Method	Materials Resources
	· Ask the Ps to calculate the summary data (PW p. 34, #11–13). This can be done as follows: o In groups (for example, asking one group to sum up the work time and another to sum up the elapsed times) o By individuals doing the same *as the times are identified* by the team members so that when the step times are completed, the summary data is almost finished · When all the times have been completed, review the work and elapsed time data with the group. Ask Ps the following: 1. Which activities use the most elapsed time? 2. Which activities use the most work time? 3. Which activities have the greatest discrepancy between the elapsed and work time? (Can mark with a red dot) Note: *You can point out that these answers can be used later in deciding which activities should be improved first (e.g., have the biggest impact on saving time, decreasing the process lead time).* · Ask *why* this discrepancy is happening and FC responses (will be used later to improve the process). · Introduce and discuss the *three Bs: batch, backlogs, and bottlenecks*. (And point to them on the map if the Ps identify these as causes.) PW p. 43. · Discuss the cascading effects of these.	

Time/Topic	Purpose and Method	Materials Resources
Notes:		
10:00–10:15 BREAK	· Meet with your practitioner team. Elicit feedback and make any course corrections.	
10:15–11:00 IDENTIFYING WASTES, THREE BS, APPLYING LEAN CONCEPTS **Eight Wastes and Lean Concepts (Five Whys) The Three Bs**	**Purpose:** · Recognize the wastes in our current state process and apply continuous improvement concepts that are effective in reducing or eliminating them. · Practice working with the continuous improvement concepts. · Incorporate using the process analysis questions. · Prepare to begin creating their future state process. **Methodology:** · Transition: Before we move into creating the future state, we want to spend a little time working with the ideas that will help you to improve the process and increase its value to the customer. Note: *Some Ps will have done the reading on waste and Lean concepts, others will not. This will give Ps a chance to get on the same page and connect these with the work.*	· Waste and concepts in PW p. 17–22 · Worksheet: Value versus Nonvalue Added HO · Worksheet: identifying wastes, root causes, and applying Lean HO

Time/Topic	Purpose and Method	Materials Resources
VA versus NVA	Review and discuss "The Eight Wastes" on PW pp. 17–18 and "Lean Concepts" on PW pp. 19–22. Briefly review/relate the "Three Bs" to these as appropriate. · Transition: Now let's look more closely at one of the Lean concepts, value added and nonvalue added. · Read the worksheet: value versus nonvalue added on PW pp. 39–40. · Ask Ps to complete the worksheet within three to five minutes. · Debrief the worksheet: VA versus NVA. o All answers are NVA except three, six, and seven, which are VA. o Statement (nine) is NVA; however, if the customer requires that one form is kept in a local office, then this activity would be 50 percent NVA. o Tell Ps that something may be NVA but necessary. Elicit examples from Ps. Teaching point: *This whole set of examples illustrates specific wastes inferring specific Lean remediation. A subsequent "learning opportunity" might capitalize on this.* · This is an important concept. Ask Ps how all these relate to their process and improving it. · If time allows, tell Ps that we are going to use these concepts we've been talking about in a practical way; ask Ps to take the "Waste Worksheet" in their PW (pp. 49–51), complete it, and return with it on day three.	

Notes:

Time/Topic	Purpose and Method	Materials Resources
11:00–Noon **Prepare for Future State Mapping—Process Analysis Questions**	**Purpose:** · Recognize the wastes in our current state process and apply continuous improvement concepts that are effective in reducing or eliminating them · Practice working with the continuous improvement concepts · Incorporate using the process analysis questions · Prepare to begin creating their future state process **Methodology:** · Briefly discuss process analysis questions (PW pp. 53–54). · BOs: Divide Ps into small groups depending on the size of the group and the size of the process being mapped. · Give Ps about forty minutes to complete the worksheets. · Ask the Ps to read the questions in the process analysis questions and record the answers. This analysis and the answers will help them in the next task and, most importantly, in creating their improved future state. · Whole Team: Debrief/round-robin the process analysis questions in the large team, having each small group report out. · Ask for commonalities and differences. Provide teaching points as appropriate.	· PW pp. 53–54: process analysis questions
Notes:		

Time/Topic	Purpose and Method	Materials Resources
12:00–12:30 LUNCH	· Meet with the staff. Elicit feedback and make any changes to improve the experience for the team. · Assess where the team is and adjust afternoon time frames accordingly. If needed, prep the VSM manager to begin thinking about the report to the sponsor.	
12:30–1:30 BEGIN FUTURE STATE MAPPING	**Purpose:** · To create a future state map that applies continuous improvement principles, moves the state of Maine toward its LTC goals, and motivates individual and team commitment and enthusiasm **Methodology:** · Have the team look at the current state as drawn; then (in preparation for mapping the future state) ask about the overall flow: o Does the flow of this process need to be changed? o Does it make sense the way it is being done now? o What is the critical path? (A *critical path* is the sequence of activities that adds up to the longest overall duration. This determines the shortest time possible to complete the process. Any delay of an activity on the critical path directly impacts the planned completion date. Steps that do not affect the duration of the process are not critical in this sense and, therefore, are of lesser priority for improvement with regard to the length of the process.) Note: *The reason these questions are being asked is in case the flow just does not make any sense to the group at all. This gives them a chance to design a new flow before going through each step.*	· Green step/action sheets · Red kaizen bursts · Yellow Post-its for clarifying notes · Blue Post-its for improvements · Pink Post-its for specific change/improvement actions for improvement. plan.

<table>
<tr><th>Time/Topic</th><th>Purpose and Method</th><th>Materials Resources</th></tr>
<tr><td>BO Groups</td><td>· Read aloud worksheet: future state mapping (PW p. 60).
· Review parking lot/improvement ideas.
· Review charter and matrix goals/outcomes as needed.
Note: Reinforce with the Ps that they are not bound by the current state—it only informs them as they create a future state.
· BO into two to three small groups and ask each group to create the future state map by starting at the beginning of the process. (PW p. 57)
1. Remind them to identify a reporter and a timekeeper.
2. Give each group a set of Post-its—each group with a different color (not the same color as the note and improvement Post-its)
3. Tell them they will have forty minutes as a group to quickly "brainstorm" a new process, writing one step per Post-it and putting it on the group's butcher paper on the wall:
a. A step should start with a verb and include a noun.
4. Tell each group to work together as a cohesive whole and not to worry about completeness or accuracy—to get their future process ideas out as quickly as possible.
5. Let them know they can suggest combining steps, eliminating steps, resequencing steps, identifying new steps, et cetera.
6. Remind them not to get bogged down in lengthy discussions—write the issue on a buff/yellow Post-it and put on a parking lot.
· Call time and ask the groups to come together as a team, bringing their maps with them and posting them up front.</td><td></td></tr>
</table>

Time/Topic	Purpose and Method	Materials Resources
Notes:		
1:30–2:15 **Continue Future State Mapping**	**Purpose:** · Continue the momentum and build consensus about the new future state. **Methodology:** · Create the future state map in the whole team by starting at the beginning of the process. · Now, with the data manager and the whole team, begin to build the future state on green data sheets, collecting measurements as each step is identified. · Starting at the beginning, use and refer to the information on the Post-its that were just done; as the team is working on each step, ask questions such as: o Is this step needed? o Can it be simplified (or combined/integrated)? o Are there Lean concepts we could apply (point to the worksheet they completed on waste)? o Ask the *five whys.* o Refer also to the blue Post-its and/or dots from current state map and incorporate them into the process where it makes sense.	

Time/Topic	Purpose and Method	Materials Resources
	· As they are doing this, ask the Ps to also think about and identify if there is a change large enough to need a separate team to meet for a day or more in order to solve the problem or another process or issue external to (but affecting) this process that must be addressed. o Be prepared to briefly explain Lean improvement methodologies/tools and what a kaizen burst is and how it differs from a VSM. · As the team works its way through the future state, ask them to briefly name these on red kaizen (rapid improvement) burst sheets and have the data manager place each burst above/below the appropriate step(s). · Continue building the future state (naming the steps and completing the data) and help the team to get as far as it can in this session. · Be sure to keep focus on the task. *Remind the Ps that this phase is about what the Ps want the future state to be, not about how to get there—* that will be done in the next session in the implementation plan. · However, tell the Ps that if they do have ideas about how to get to the future state, to write each one down on a bright pink Post-it and put that on the appropriate step at the end of the session.	
Notes:		

Time/Topic	Purpose and Method	Materials Resources
2:15–2:30 BREAK	· Meet with your practitioner team. Elicit feedback and make any course corrections.	
2:30–3:45 FINISH FUTURE STATE MAPPING	**Purpose:** · Continue the momentum and build consensus of a new, improved future state. **Methodology:** · Same	
NOTES:		
3:45–4:15 CALCULATE FUTURE STATE TIMES	**Purpose:** · Measure the projected improvements from current state to future state · Reinforce the value of using data when identifying improvement opportunities **Methodology:** · Same as current state. See *Day One Design Notes.* · Tell Ps to use PW pp. 34–36if thry need a reminder. The calculation is the same as for the current state. o Remind Ps that when there are simultaneous steps, they should calculate the process (lead) elapsed time, and use the longest times. · When completed, review the differences/similarities/patterns between the CS and FS.	

Time/Topic	Purpose and Method	Materials Resources
NOTES:		
4:15–4:30 WRAP UP AND AD-JOURN	**Purpose:** · Acknowledge the work completed and give appreciation to each other. · Invite Ps to prepare for day three—read the improvement plan questions. **Methodology:** · Practitioner summarizes work completed and action items for next session. Asks team to think about how they would actually get from the current state to the future state—what would have to be done. · Checkout**:** Round-robin, ask Ps, for example, one of the following: o Give a word or a sentence about what they appreciate about the work *the team* has completed over the past two days. o Say, in a phrase or sentence, what key or "Aha!" learning they had today. · When the last person has spoken, you will be adjourned.	

Time/Topic	Purpose and Method	Materials Resources
NOTES:		

Questions for Analyzing the Current State of Your Process in Order to Make Improvements*		
1	A. Functions	
2	Can the number of functions (departments, work units, or individuals) be reduced? (If so, consider using their talents and capacity to provide the additional services for which you have not had the needed resources.)	
3	Which movements between functions could be eliminated or the distance/time decreased?	
4	B. Activities	
5	Which activities offer the greatest potential for improvements?	
6	Which steps are unnecessary and could be eliminated?	
7	Will changing the sequence of the steps result in greater efficiency?	
8	C. Time	
9	Which activities consume the most elapsed time?	
10	Which activities consume the most work time?	
11	Which activities show the greatest discrepancy between work time and elapsed time?	
12	Based on the previous three answers, which activities should be improved first for the greatest reduction in elapsed and work time?	
13	How can time be saved on critical path activities? (The critical path is the series of tasks/activities/steps that must be completed as scheduled to produce the final product in the time planned—the path of longest duration. Time saved on noncritical path activity has no effect on the elapsed time for the whole process.)	

14	Which activities could be done in parallel to reduce total elapsed time?	
15	D. Batch Processing	
16	Where does batch processing occur?	
17	What is its impact on elapsed time?	
18	Can reducing the batch size improve elapsed time?	
19	E. Inspections/Approvals	
20	Where do inspections/approval by third parties occur?	
21	Why are inspections/approvals done? What is the inspector's/approver's real reason for needing to see the product or information about it?	
22	How else could this need be addressed?	
23	Can the inspections/approvals be made unnecessary?	
24	F. Yield/Volume	
25	At what points (activities/steps) should the yield be checked?	
26	How can the actual yield be measured and charted?	
27	How can the yield be increased?	
28	G. Variation	
29	Where does variability occur in the process (that is, something that necessitates exception processing or special handling)?	
30	H. Rework	
31	Where do rework or correction cycles occur?	
32	How can this rework be eliminated or reduced?	
33	Where do errors occur in the process?	
34	How can these errors be reduced?	

35	What can be done earlier in the process to eliminate rework?	
36	I. Cost	
37	Which activities represent the greatest cost?	
38	How can the cost be reduced?	
39	J. Complexity	
40	Where does the process seem unnecessarily complex?	
41	How can it be simplified?	
42	K. Customer Contact	
43	Where are customers given an "I don't know" answer?	
44	Where can responsiveness to customers be improved?	
45	Where can the "friendliness" of customer contact (face-to-face, paper, electronic, et cetera) be improved?	
46	Where can information be given to customers to shape their expectations?	
47	How can the number and duration of contact points be reduced / simplified?	

* Adapted from Ken Miller *The Change Agent's Guide to Radical Improvement* (Milwaukee, WI.: ASQ Press, 2002), 142–143.

Questions to Consider in Developing the Improvement Action Plan

- What are the changes being proposed?
- Which changes should be implemented first?
  - Which problems/changes are priorities for OCFS? For the child?
  - Which changes address key organizational goals?
- What specific actions/activities must be taken to bring them about successfully?
- How will the changes be implemented?
- Who is the staff person responsible for implementing the change successfully—who has the commitment, authority, influence, and time to assure implementation, to remove barriers to change?
- What are the measures needed to determine if the changes are successful? To determine if they're actually improvements?
  - How will it be determined if the changes are seen as actual improvements by the child, the adoptive parents, and by staff?
- How will input from clients, staff, and external sources be obtained regarding possible improvements, best practices, et cetera.
- How will any adjustments be made to the proposed changes if they are found not to work or to be actual improvements after all?
- Are there any significant problems related to this process that must be addressed in order to get to the future state for this process?
- Are there any changes, barriers, other processes, or issues outside this process that must also be addressed in order to get to the future state for this process?

APPENDIX C

Improvement Intervention Charter—Example

<u>Intervention/Process Name</u>: Allocation Plans and Work Programs			
Name	**Position/Job**	**Phone**	**Email**
Sponsor:	Director, Program and Fiscal Coordination and Division of Purchased Services (PFC and DPS)		
Manager: M H	Director, Division of Purchased Services (DPS)		
Team Members:	Director, PFC and DPS Director, DPS Program Fiscal Coordinator Program Fiscal Coordinator Program Fiscal Coordinator Deputy Director, Service Center Managing Staff Accountant Financial Analyst Operation Manager Purchased Services Manager Purchased Services Manager Purchased Services Manager Agreement Administrator Deputy Director, Service Center Budget Analyst MaineCare Maine CDC Adult Mental Health Child and Family Services OIT Systems Section Manager		
Data Manager:	Operations Manager		
Caucus Members:	Deputy Commissioner Director, Service Center		
CIP/Facilitators:			

Process Description: Develop electronic allocation planning documents that contain the information required to create contracts.

Customers/Clients: Division of Purchased Services, direct care providers, and other vendors.

Suppliers (upstream): Office Directors, Program Managers, Service Center Managing Staff Accountants, Program Fiscal Coordinators, Purchased Services Managers, and Agreement Administrators.

Process Boundaries—First Step:	Last Step:
Program Directors identify desired services. This may involve a review of prior period allocation plans and work programs, including contract amounts and terms, and an assessment of service-provider (vendor) performance. Seek to answer these questions: For which services are contracts required? Is funding available? How will the funds be provided?	Completed contract allocation plans are delivered to the Division of Purchased Services, and data are successfully loaded (entered) into the state's accounting system.

Problem Statement: Allocation plans are rarely completed on time and often contain significant errors or omissions. This problem results in poorly constructed work programs and departmental budgets, which create allotment issues that necessitate financial orders and delay payments to vendors.

Measurement Targets:	**Specific Measurements:**	**Timeframe:**
VSM:		
1. Reduce cycle time of the allocation planning process	The process for development of the new fiscal year allocation plans and work programs begins in February and is completed by June 30.	Five months
2. Simplify the process flow	Reduce the number of process steps by 50 percent.	
Project:		
1. Improve the collection and availability of project implementation information	Project status reports are updated and remain current each week.	
2. Reduce rework and errors, improving the quality of the work.	Reduce the number of allocation plan revisions (versions) by 90 percent. Reduce the number of budget orders due to allotment issues by 80 percent.	

3. Reduce the staff time required to provide service in order to free up resources for other work.	Reduce staff time by 75 percent.	

Resources Available: Program Managers, Managing Staff Accountants, Program Fiscal Coordinators, Purchased Services Managers, Agreement Administrators
Role Expectations: Russ Begin has oversight responsibilities for the Divisions of Program and Fiscal Coordination and Purchased Services, and he acts as liaison between the department's office directors, DHHS finance, and the DAFS service center. Team members will advocate on behalf of their stakeholders and will facilitate implementation of any resulting action plans with them.

Intervention and Project Deliverables:

Objectives	Expected Deliverables	Time Frame
Intervention Deliverables:		
1. Facilitate team analysis of the present allocation planning process	Create a process map of the current state for developing allocation plans	First day
2. Facilitate team analysis of the methods by which work programs are developed	Create a process map of the current state for developing work programs	First day
3. Simplify the process	Identify opportunities to combine duplicative efforts in the development of allocation plans and work programs	
4. Facilitate team design of a standardized process for future development of allocation plans and work programs	Create a process map of the future state	
5. Facilitate team development of an action plan to implement identified process improvements	Produce an implementation plan	
6. Facilitate two follow-up sessions within sixty days	Provide status updates and reports Identify barriers to implementation	December 2007; January 2008;

7. Facilitate a kick-off meeting for implementation of the new plan		February 2008
Project Deliverables:		
1. Product design and definitions	What is an *allocation plan*? What data elements does it contain? What is a *work program*? What does it look like? What purpose does it serve?	First day
2. Develop and implement a standardized process	Create a project plan, establish milestones, and define roles and responsibilities	
3. Allocation plans are delivered to the Division of Purchased Services	Data loaded into EIS database and entered into accounting system	June 2008
4. Evaluate the effectiveness of the new process; make changes to improve efficiency, effectiveness, and quality; identify areas for improvement		August 2008

Improvement Intervention Charter: Definitions, Descriptions, and Examples

Intervention/Process Name: A brief name for the process for which the intervention is being conducted. The charter describes the specific process and work that the team is about to address.

Intervention Team:

Sponsor: The person with overall responsibility for the intervention and its implementation.

Manager: The person responsible for managing the successful implementation of the intervention, as well as a brief outline of their authority.

Team Members: All the intervention Team members—the staff who actually do the work.

Data Manager: The person who will be responsible for assisting the other team members to calculate and track the measurements. The data manager is a part of the team.

Caucus Group Members: The resource staff members who can be called on for specific expertise or other support as needed. These members should be kept routinely informed with regard to the work and progress of the intervention.

Process Description: A brief description of the process being proposed for improvement.

Customer(s): Identifies the customer(s)/clients of this process, both internal and external to the process itself.

Supplier: The internal and/or external persons/entities that provide information, documents, supplies, people, et cetera for the process and any step within it.

Boundaries of this Process: Defines very *specifically* where this process begins and ends for the purposes of this intervention.

Problem Statement: The reason(s) you want to change this process. What you want to change, improve, or create.

Measurements: (See examples below)

Measurement Targets	Specific Measurements	Time Frame
Measurements 1. Reduce the time it takes for the whole process. 2. Simplify the process flow. 3. Reduce errors and rework, improving the quality of the work. 4. Reduce the staff time required in order to free up resources for other work. 5. Reduce associated costs, increasing savings available for improving services. **Project/Process Measurements** 1. Increase the number of customers served in a timely way. 2. Improve the collection and availability of project implementation/measurement data/information.	1. Reduce the lead time by ____ percent. 2. Reduce the number of process steps by ____ percent. 3. Increase the first pass yield percent by ____ percent. 4. Reduce staff time by ____ percent. 5. Decrease changeover time by ____ percent. 1 a. Increase the number of customers served within one week of request by ____ percent. 1 b. Over time, consistently continue to increase the number of customers served in a timely way by at least ____ percent. 1 c. Over time, consistently continue to decrease the actual amount of time spent waiting by customers after request by at least ____ percent. 2 a. All project data is updated and current on a daily basis. 2 b.	inety days Thirty days Sixty days Thirty days Thirty days Ninety days Monthly Monthly Sixty days

Resources/Budget: Identifies human, fiscal, and other resources available to the project team and project process.

Role Expectations: Describes expectations about authority and responsibility in relation to the intervention, decision-making, and implementation.

Project Deliverables: Concise description of project deliverables expected (see examples below).

Objectives	Expected Deliverables	Time Frame
Deliverables		
1. Facilitate team to analyze current process state.	1. Production of a current state map	First day
2. Facilitate team analysis of current state to identify process improvements.	2. Production of a future state map	Second day
3. Facilitate team development of an action/change plan to implement identified improvements.	3. Production of an implementation plan	Third day
4. Facilitate one or more follow-up session(s) within ninety days	4. Status updates, reports, identification of barriers to improvement	Ninety days
Project/Process Deliverables		
1. Assure implementation of the plan.	1 a. Project plan developed 1 b. Future state fully implemented	
2. Evaluate effectiveness of changes for efficiency, effectiveness, and quality and to identify needed areas of improvement.	2. Analyze, track, and report customer and program/process outcomes	
3. Develop and implement a standardized process.	3. SOP handbook/manual	
4. Assure that every program area and all staff understand what is required.	4 a. SOP developed, published, and available/accessible to all staff 4 b. SOP training developed and required	

APPENDIX D

Certification Checklist

This certification record is designed to track and document completion of all requirements necessary to perform as a practitioner for continuous improvement events (chartering teams, value stream mapping, process flow mapping, kaizen, problem-solving, team planning). Each space should be initialed and dated by a certified CIP. The new practitioner should keep this list until complete. When complete, it is passed on to the *BTC* manager/director for your agency.

Practitioners who are not certified must partner with other practitioners until they are cleared on all the items in this list and it is documented by *BTC*.

	Initials	Date
Preentry		
· Participate in Five-Day Introductory Development of CIP (DOP1)		
· Observe two two/three-day VSM		
· Observe a two-day kaizen		
· Colead two VSMs/kaizens		
· Lead two VSM/kaizens.		
· Participate in the five-day DOP2		
· Complete CIP written exam with at least 90 percent accuracy (see attached)		
· Submit complete portfolio of all work and requirements		
· Score "acceptable" on all areas of competency list (see attached)		
Administrative and Logistics		
· Demonstrate initiative and follow through with logistics and administrative processes associated with the work: o Arrange for room if needed o Arrange for snacks and lunch if needed o Ensure communication to participants is clear and timely o Ensure room is arranged properly and materials and equipment are available		
Chartering		

· Initiate and lead a chartering meeting with sponsor and VSM manager; all key elements of the charter are clarified and the form is completed		
· CI practitioner leaves contracting meeting with no unanswered questions · A shared understanding of all the elements of the charter "template": o Outcomes o Deliverables o Identified customer(s) of the process to be mapped o Goals o Problem statement that is quantifiable o Boundaries ▪ "Bookends" of the process to be mapped ▪ Roles clarified · Membership of the team: Have we got the right people on the team? o Who's here? Who's missing? o Do we have the "knowledge" present of the entire process? · Hold VSM as close to work site as possible (so can go verify information if needed)		
VSM		
· Complete the room setup before the team arrives a) Projector and laptop hooked up and working (or flip charts arranged) b) Butcher paper or flip chart paper put on wall for map c) Chairs and tables arranged as appropriate d) Handouts arranged for each team member		
Start-Up		
· Introductions, ground rules, agenda, logistics o What participants need to feel safe and welcomed		
· Review the roles of each of the team members, ensuring that each member is clear about what is expected		
· If it was not completed earlier, ask for and assign a data manager		
· Review the charter—clarify the purpose (this is a review, not a revisit)		
· Review the materials going to be working with		

· Decide on decision-making process		
Process Flow—Beginning to End—Brainstorm		
· Read Worksheet: Current State Flow to the room.		
· In large print, write the first step and last step of the process (the bookends, boundary) as agreed to in the charter.		
· Using Post-it notes, have each team member internally brainstorm and write each step on separate Post-it notes, then one at a time go to the front of the room and quickly place the Post-its in the order, reading them aloud as they place them.		
· Have team quickly organize the Post-its with a flow, beginning to end, within the boundaries that were set in the charter. **Note**: Because there is no standard, you may have more than one process embedded in the brainstorm. Do not get hung up. This is a quick activity and is not intended to be perfect or accurate.		
· Give the data manager the current state data sheets (usually buff colored) and a Sharpie and ask the data manager to fill in the name of the step in large bold print as the team identifies the step.		
Presentation #1		
· Give the approved VSM presentation and present it to the VSM team while using the correct terminology and definitions of the steps, data, and measurements · Vocabulary o Use words and language that fit the service sector · Value added and nonvalue added · Measurements and how to calculate them · Use examples that reflect the experience of the group · Be aware of the audience and if they are with you or not · Why? What is the purpose of doing this in the context of state government? · Attend to different learning styles · Use supportive learning aids (charts, visuals, et cetera)		
· Complete Worksheet: Value Added		
Map Current State—End to Beginning		
· Read Worksheet: Current State Mapping to the room.		
· Starting at the end, with the <u>customer</u>, ask the team what the step just before the boundary is and have the data manager enter the name of the step and then tape the data sheet on the map.		

· The facilitator now fills in each data box of the data sheet while facilitating the team to arrive at the correct data. (Allow discussions to take place for a reasonable time. If at the work site, gather real data if appropriate.) Note: Before signing off on this step, ensure that the practitioner is applying the correct definitions of the data.		
· Using Post-it notes, other than pink colored, place any pertinent notes near the data sheet (such as why the CO is so long, UT is low, et cetera).		
· Working from right to left, continue to list each step, no matter how small, on the data sheets and complete each data box.		
· Once all data sheets are completed, step back and have the team identify any areas that should be highlighted (low UT, high CO, et cetera) and highlight in a bright color.		
Current State Data Calculations		
· Add the cycle time (CT) from each data sheet and write it at the end of the process. This is the *lead time* for the process. Example: Cycle Time #1 + Cycle Time #2 + Cycle Time #3, et cetera = LT = two hundred minutes		
· Add the staff time (ST) from each data sheet and write that at the end of the process. This is the *staff time* for the process. Example: Staff Time #1 + Staff Time #2 + Staff Time #3, et cetera = ST = one hundred minutes		
· Calculate the *value-added time* for each step by multiplying the cycle time (CT) by the value-added (VA) percent and write that number on each data sheet. Example: VA percent x CT = VA minutes = 25 percent x one hundred minutes = twenty-five VA minutes		
· Add the *value-added time* from all data sheets and divide this number by the lead time calculated in step one above. Calculate the percent VA by multiplying the result by one hundred to get percent. Example: Total VA 50 minutes = 0.25 x 100 = 25 percent Lead time two hundred minutes		
· Calculate the *nonvalue-added (NVA) time* by subtracting the value added percent from 100 percent. Example: 100 percent – 25 percent = 75 percent NVA		
· Count the number of steps (data sheets) and write at the end of the process. Example: eighteen steps		

· Have the team carefully study each data sheet—mark any data that really stands out, for example: o Inventory that is much higher than the other data sheets/steps o Uptime that is much lower than the others o Change over that is much higher than the others o FPY that is lower than 95 percent o Low value-added percentage If so, mark that step so you will not miss it the next day for improvement considerations during the future state—circle that piece of data with a marker or use a small Post-it to point it out.		
· The data should be for one piece, document, or case, et cetera. Multiply the *lead time* by the *total cycles*, documents, et cetera that are done in a day, a week, and finally in a year. Write this down at the end of the process map—in pencil for now. Example: Total documents in a day = 30 Total documents in a week = 150 Total documents in a year = 7800		
· Now do the above step again for the staff time—total *staff time* multiplied by the total cycles in a year.		
Presentation #2: Future State		
· Give the approved presentation #2		
· Key concepts include:		
Future State Mapping		
· Read Worksheet: Future State Mapping		
· Give the future state data sheets (light green) to the data manager, and starting at the beginning of the process this time, ask the question, "Is this step still needed?" If so, then have the data manager fill out the name of the step and tape the sheet under the current state map. Note: Focus on where there is the greatest amount of waste.		
· Have the team determine the data as it will be in the future state, and facilitator fills in all of the data boxes of each future state step.		
· Using Post-it notes, other than pink, put any pertinent data near the data sheets.		
· Using *pink* Post-it notes (brighter is better), place any suggestions for improvement under the data sheet.		

· If it is felt that the suggested improvements need any of the following, then use a red kaizen burst: o A team and a full day or two to develop the implementation plan is needed. o The root cause of the problem is not known, and in order to develop a plan, a root cause analysis will be needed.		
· Repeat the above steps until the end of the process.		
Future State Calculations		
· To collect the data for the Future State, do the same steps you did for the *current state data calculations* above.		
Final Data Calculations		
· Subtract the *future state lead time* from the *current state lead time* and write it on the map at the end using a marker and label *lead time reduction.*		
· Subtract the *future staff time* from the *current staff time* and write it on the map at the end using a marker and label *staff time reduction.*		
· Subtract the *future state NVA* from the *current state NVA* and write it on the map at the end using a market and label *NVA reduction.*		
· Subtract the *future state number of steps* from the *current state number of steps* and write it on the map at the end using a marker and label *step reduction.*		
· Write current state info and future state info on the metrics template.		
· Multiply the staff time reduction by 0.58 to arrive at the total yearly $ saved by going to the future state.		
Value Stream Map Implementation Plan (Excel Spreadsheet)		
· Write the name of the process you are working on at the top of the spreadsheet.		
· Write all the ideas from the pink Post-its and the kaizen bursts from the future state map in the "recommendation" column.		
· Ask for volunteers or select a responsible person for each recommendation and add to plan.		
· Select a due date for each recommendation and add to plan—remember that the due date is not necessarily the date the change will be complete. It may be the date the evaluation of the recommendation is complete.		

· Fill in the *estimated gains* (est. gains) for each recommendation: a) The change in time from the current state step to the future state step b) Any gains from material reduction—paper, printer ink, et cetera c) Any gains from reduction in postage, envelopes, et cetera d) Any gains from reduction of forms used, et cetera e) Equate staff time savings at fifty-eight cents per minute in the absence of more specific data f) Equate FTEs at 98,400 minutes per FTE in the absence of more specific data		
· Fill in the estimated *days (or hours) saved per year* (SVD/YR)		
· Fill in the estimated *dollars saved per year* ($ SAVED/YR)		
· Total estimated gains, days saved, and dollars saved columns		
Kaizen (To Be Developed)		

Notes:

APPENDIX E

Development of Facilitators Certification Exam

Section 1:

1. Name at least five differences between the administrative/service sector and the industrial sector:

2. True or false: All work is a process.
   a. Why is it _____ (true or false)?

3. Work that exclusively involves people is so unique that it does not fit this definition of a process: "A process is a combination of people, resources, and methods, which produces a result."
   a. True or false?
   b. Why?

4. What are the five ways in which the administrative/service sector is the *same* as the industrial sector?

5. "Everything can be improved," "that that is measured tends to improve," and "perfection has not been achieved yet" are all illustrations of which of the following?
   a. Continues improvement
   b. Customer satisfaction
   c. A process working well so don't touch it
   d. If it ain't broke, don't fix it
   e. None of the above
6. If *all* problems happen for a reason, which of the following does not fit?
   a. If it isn't broke, don't fit it
   b. There are causes for everything
   c. Finding the (root) cause of a problem creates meaningful and lasting improvement

7. It has been empirically demonstrated that the cost of the service sector, banking, government, health care, retail, et cetera is inflated by 30 between 80 percent, how would you rank the following as major causes (one being the highest value)?
    a. Work not thought of as a process
    b. Processes not defined and followed
    c. Methods not standardized
    d. Processes not measured
    e. Customer needs not being well defined
    f. Systematic problem-solving not used

8. From the above, if you ranked "Customer needs not being well defined" as your number one choice, explain why. If you ranked "Customer needs not being well defined" as another rank (other than number one), explain why.

9. When delivering an MDOL or a DHHS service, or a product, is it ever the case that you are correct (or right) and the customer is wrong? Give a quick example.

10. Can you envision a day, if it's not today, when you would think it a fun thing to do to think of all of your work as being a process? Briefly explain.

Section 2

1. Give three examples of a changeover activity in a service or office environment.

2. What is cycle time?
    a. The time it takes the entire process to be completed
    b. The time from the beginning of the prior step to the beginning of the current step
    c. The time from the end of the last step to the end of the current step
    d. The time from the beginning of the current step to the end of the current step

3. What is one of the duties of a value stream manager?
    a. Develop the problem statement for the value stream
    b. Update the VSM plan as progress is made for the value stream
    c. Facilitate the value stream mapping event
    d. Ensure evaluation sheets for each VSM event are filled out and routed to management

4. What is the definition of waste as related to Lean implementation?

5. What is the purpose of value stream mapping the current state of the process?

6. In the data box of the VSM data sheet, what does FPY mean? Include a definition.

7. How is FPY calculated?

8. There are two types of *muda* or waste. What are the two types?

9. Of the two types of *muda* or waste, which one should be eliminated first?

10. When the team is drawing the future state map, what should they be focusing on?

11. If the inventory prior to a step is thirty-five items and the cycle time of the step is five minutes, what is the time related to the inventory?

12. What is the definition of *lead time*?

13. How is lead time of a process calculated?

14. Which of the following are measurements that would be an outcome of a value stream mapping event? (Circle all that are correct.)
    a. Potential number of steps reduced by the future state map
    b. Potential number of *personnel* hours reduced by the future state
    c. Potential reduction of lead time for a process
    d. Potential postage savings

15. How are the tasks chosen for action during the VSM event tracked to completion?

16. Why is it important to allow the people that do the work every day to participate in the improvement process, generate the ideas for improvement, and implement them, rather than doing it for them?

17. What is 5S? List each one and give an explanation of what it is.

18. What is the difference between the perceived problem and the root cause of the problem?

19. How would you get past the perceived problem and arrive at the root cause?

20. What is a pull system?

21. What do standards provide? (Circle all that apply.)
    a. A document that can be used as a training tool for employees
    b. A document that will help ensure that each process will be done the same way by all
    c. A springboard for future improvements
    d. A method to ensure consistent quality for each process

22. Which of the following is an example of an *andon*?
    a. An email alerting you that you have a new or revised procedure to review or approve
    b. A procedure that lists step by step how to do a specific process
    c. A piece of paper used during the VSM event that lists all the data for the step
    d. A method of transferring human intelligence to machines

23. Which of the following is one of the deliverables of a kaizen event?
    a. A guarantee of specific financial gains
    b. A package that documents every step of the ten-step process
    c. A specific culture change throughout the organization
    d. A method to eliminate all required *muda*

24. One of the goals of the kaizen mandate or charter is to define the boundaries

of the kaizen event. Why is it important for all team members to know those boundaries?

25. Kaizen team should be composed of members from what areas as related to the kaizen? Why?

26. During a kaizen event, actual changes should be made if possible. Why is this important?

27. What is the kaizen storyboard used for? (Circle all that apply.)
    a. A guide for the kaizen team as they proceed with the kaizen event
    b. A device used to measure all of the gains in the VSM
    c. A tool to use for presenting the kaizen outcome to management
    d. It is used to do the initial kaizen presentation to the kaizen team

28. What is the definition of "value added"?

29. How is value-added time determined for each step of the process?

30. How is nonvalue-added time calculated for the entire process?

31. How are kaizen events identified on the map during a VSM future state mapping event?

APPENDIX F

Sample Study Mission Questions

Questions	Answer
• How does your organization keep the Lean/problem-solving momentum going? • How does it keep constantly changing and improving the process?	
• What strategies, training, et cetera, do you use for staff incentives?	
• What metrics do you have that show that you are making progress? • What was your baseline?	
• What is your Lean infrastructure? • How do you make it happen? • Do you have examples of its application in administrative settings, as well as on the operational end?	
• How was Lean introduced at your organization? • What are strategies you use to become a Lean organization while continuing daily operations? • Transitioning? • Thoughts about pushing employees to "learn the Lean language?"	
• Any negative impacts, such as feedback from employees? • How is this dealt with?	
• What are the positives? (Ex. process flexibility)	
• Under what circumstances do you fix a product and move it on versus halt the work and fix the process?	
• How did you do the initial education to get people on board with Lean? • What do you do to keep the learning going?	
• What Lean tools do you use?	
• Average time from start to finish of Lean initiatives (i.e., achieving desired future state)?	
• Is Lean used in this specific unit/area only or is it statewide?	

APPENDIX G

MDOL *BTC* Strategic Plan

The code name of the Program was Bend the Curve (i.e., literally, bend the expense curve so that it matches the funds curve).

- Strategy:
  - Be customer focused
  - Provide high-quality service and products
  - Be an efficient and effective provider of services and products
    - Reduce costs
    - Decrease lead time
    - Measurable continuous improvement
- Goal:
  - Provide the same or better service
  - Shift the work of the department to match customer expectations and needs
  - Achieve efficiencies by fundamentally changing how work gets done
  - Improve interdepartmental collaboration and service integration
  - Decrease expenditures by $9 million of a $47 million operating budget and significantly reduce staffing levels over three years while minimizing layoffs.

- Staffing the Initiative:
  - Program leader: commissioner
  - Executive director: deputy commissioner
  - Program designer, planner, and manager: executive director of operations
    - Assisted by: department's budget manager
    - Statistician: department's statistician
  - Senior leaders: department's bureau/division directors
  - Management team: managers, supervisors, lead persons, and comparable organize labor employees.

- Establish a proof of concept (i.e., a pilot) as an initial element of the consulting engagement. Conduct no less than two pilots.

The Plan

A. Overarching Objective: Transform how the department leads, plans, executes, coach, directs, and manages how work gets accomplished. For three reasons, hire two private sector consultants to assist Arthur in implementing the "Lean Production Applied in the Maine Department of Labor Plan": an organizational development expert (ODE) and a Lean production expert (LPE). Make the ODE the lead consultant. Why? From Arthur's past experience, he discovered the following:

1. It is too often the case that the LPE has limited to no appreciation, knowledge, and skill of what's required to fundamentally transform an organization. And all too often, they are blinded by the technological solution that they espouse as being capable of making a fundamental change to include transforming an organization.
2. On the other hand, it is often the case that the ODE is steeped in the knowledge required to transform an organization. However, they are most practiced at facilitating an organization and a manner that enables them to discover, for themselves, the most acceptable and effective leadership and management style/method to give them the greatest benefit for their investment (i.e., they help organizations discover, as opposed to take advantage of, a superior leadership, management, and execution system.
3. And a third reason that Arthur hired external consultants is this: as an internal operative, it is infinitely more difficult to lead your colleagues in a place that they've never been. It's not impossible, but it is very problematic. They've seen you in action; they know that up to this point you have espoused the same belief and value system that they have espoused and/or operated with. For you to wake up one morning and say that he has a new set of beliefs and values just simply does not work. So even though he had many of the skills necessary to lead a transformative change within the organization. Thus, he recommended hiring reading external consultants.

B. Bend the Curve (*BTC*) initiative—rollout, transformation, and creating "a way of life"

1. The rollout: What it is? Why and how to roll out?

a. What is a "rollout"? A disciplined, standardized process used to introduce, inform, explain, and ask/answer questions, so as to ensure transparency, what *BTC* is, what caused its use, and why and what MDOL will do about it.
b. Why is a "rollout" necessary? There are at least two schools of thought as regards starting a "large system change." Some say start in a small and manageable manner. The other approach is to involve the whole system. The MDOL chose the "whole system" approach.
    i. Why not the "start small and manageable" approach? This is one of the best answers to this question. Have you ever played the "telephone" game (or Chinese whispers)? If you have, you are well on your way to knowing why this is not as solid a recommendation as it first seems. Briefly, as the games ends, the beginning utterance or message in unrecognizable.
    ii. Why the whole system approach? One must use methods that get *everyone* in the system *included in making the change a reality*. In other words, getting them to see themselves having not only survived the change but "coming out the other end" of the change in a personally better place than when they entered.

2. Transformation/creating "a way of life"
    a. Create a monthly leadership and management training event.
    b. Immediately upon completion of the department-wide rollout event(s), engage a statistically significant element of MDOL in the act of applying Lean to solve real problems.

        Note: Broadcast the results.

        - *First and foremost, know that you (leaders) are going to implement the ideas proposed by the improvement teams' ideas.*
        - Develop a process for selecting improvement projects.
        - All projects must be measured and their results reported in a timely fashion
        - Develop a process for team selection.
        - Develop a formal project review process.

c. Develop an MDOL-wide *BTC* "fair" for teams to share their process improvement successes.
d. Become self-sufficient (virtually free of consulting support) in two and a half years or less.
e. Develop and implement a Lean practitioner training course in not more than six months after starting the *BTC* initiative.
    - The training course should have at least two stages: the beginner practitioner and "an experience practitioner." And both of these should be certifiable based on "Lean marketplace" certifying criteria.

Maine Department of Labor
Bend-The-Curve (BTC) – Project Team Performance
2004 to 2007 (From Initial Start- Up to 2 ½ Years Before MDOL's BTC's End)

Maine Department of Labor 's Sub-groups	Type of Intervention (e.g. Pilot) and/or Location the Intervention was Conducted	Name of the Process	Identified[1] Savings	Staff Minutes Mapped
Bureau of Employment Services (BES)	Pilot	Job Order	$0[2]	
BES	Pilot	Job Match	$0	
BES	Continued from Pilot	Job Order/Job Match	$3,160,767	0
Bureau of Rehabilitation Services (BRS)	Pilot	R-20 Payment Process	$0	0
Pilot Total			$3,160,767	
LMIS = now Center for Workforce Research and Information (CWRI)	Location of the Improvement Intervention: China Lake, November 2004	WIN-202 Continuous Improvement	$574,373	0
Bureau of Unemployment Compensation (BUC)	China Lake, November 2004	UI Tax and Benefit collections, Update Garnishment	$466,673	115,700
BUC	China Lake, November 2004	UI Tax and Benefit collections, Tax Payment 1 of 2	$109,151	17,100
BUC	China Lake, November 2004	UI Tax and Benefit collections, Monthly Statement of Accounts	$2,298,055	300,000

1 Cost savings reflect annual staff time saved, calculated in minutes using an average per minute cost of $.58 per minute. Not all cost savings are included (i.e. impact on the work of other staff, paper saved, postage saved, mileage, etc.).

2 It was rare that an improvement team found no improvement. Most likely a 0 was an indication of other factors. Such as: distrust of the improvement tool(s) and/or the process; newness of the participants and/or the process leader, or the leader of the work unit, etc.

BUC	China Lake, November 2004	UI Tax and Benefit collections, Elimination of write-off notice	$172,433	26,000
BUC	China Lake, November 2004	UI Tax and Benefit collections, Electronic Bankruptcy Noticing	$683,362	104,000
BUC	China Lake, November 2004	UI Tax and Benefit collections, Benefit Repayment	$0	32,637
Admin. Office of the Department of Labor (DOL)	China Lake, November 2004	Publications Distribution(internal/ external)	$329,045	0
Department of Admin. & Financial Ser. (DAFS)	China Lake, November 2004	Procurement and Accounts Payable (Accounts Payable)	$187,040	162,000
DOL	China Lake, November 2004	Outreach and Education	$0	0
DOL	China Lake, November 2004	OIP Job Jar	$528,020	2,155,600
BRS	China Lake, November 2004	Increase SSA/VR Reimbursements	$3,023,014	0
BUC	China Lake, November 2004	Fact-finding & Appeals	$0	8,750,000
BRS	China Lake, November 2006	Improve Voc Rehab Service Delivery	$0	821,583
BRS	China Lake, November 2007	BRS Job Development	$0	4,097,950
DOL	China Lake, November, 2004	Website	$1,359,348	365,000
DOL	China Lake, November, 2004	Empowerment & Decision Making	$773,915	0
Location of the Improvement Intervention: China Lake Total			$10,504,428	16,947,570
DAFS	Location of the Improvement Intervention: St Paul Center, March 2005	Integrated Financial Management System	$0	0
BUC	St Paul Center, March 2005	Admin Support Services for BUC, DAH & UIC	$0	0

DAFS	St Paul Center, March 2006	Travel	$0	0
DAFS	St Paul Center, March, 2005	Comprehensive Budget & Planning	$0	1,349,585
St Paul Center Total			$0	1,349,585
BUC		Seasonal Dates Automation	$0	
BUC		Initial Claims	$0	0
BES		Employment and Training Services	$0	
DOL		Employer Audits	$0	
DOL		DOL Relocation	$0	
DOL		Common Intake	$0	0
BUC		BUC Special Projects (As of 1/9/2007)	$854,243	
Bureau of Labor Standards (BLS)	2006	Service Delivery for Migrant, Seasonal, and Foreign Certified Workers	$313,237	168,700
DAFS	2006	Selection And Recruitment	$0	
DAFS	2006	Performance Management	$0	
BLS	2006	Migrant, Seasonal, and Foreign Certified Workers Administration Activities	$0	
BLS	2006	Migrant Seasonal Farm Workers	$0	
DAFS	2006	Procurement and Accounts Payable (Procurement)	$0	0
BES	2008	GTI Application Process	$140,100	
BLS	May-07	BLS Coding Project	$59,208	29,400

DAFS/DOL	2008	Federal reporting		
BES	May-09	BES Case Management		
BES	Mar-07	BES Bangor Local Office		
DOL	Jun-06	Common Functions Kaizen	$0	
Other (not named above) Maine Department of Labor Initiatives Total			$28,697,178	36,792,410
BTC TOTAL (first two and half years).			$39,201,606	55,+89,565

Developed: Statistician John Rioux
Maine Department of Labor
John created, established, managed, and maintained

State of Maine

VSM Materials Lists – “Kits”

This is the list of supplies and materials required for each VSM team. It is the responsibility of the facilitator to review the team's kit and be sure all the materials are there.

Item	Color	Size	AMT	Day
Pre-Printed Materials				
VSM Participants' Workbook *Agenda - Customized to group*			One for each team member	
Copy of team's Charter			One for each team member	1
*VSM Data Sheets - Current State**	Buff or light yellow	5 1/2 X 8 1/2**	at least 36	1
*VSM Data Sheets - Future State**	Light Green paper	5 1/2 X 8 1/2**	at least 36	2
*Kaizen Burst Sheets**	Red paper	Letter	5	Both
Name Tags			One for each team member	Both
Flip Charts, 'Wall Paper'				
Flip Chart Paper or Rolls of Paper, butcher paper to Line Walls			Make sure to have plenty	Both
Flip Chart Pad and stand			1	Both
Materials, Supplies				
Post-its	Yellow, Blue, Dark Pink	4 X 4	One pad for each team member	Both
Self stick Dots	Red and Yellow	3/4 inch	At least 20	Both
Calculator			One for each team	Both
Pencils			3	Both
Masking Tape			Make sure to have plenty	Both
VSM Name of the Process Step (White paper)	Plain White paper	Letter	at least 36	1
Flip Chart Markers	Different colors		Several	Both
Sharpie Pens			One for each team member	Both
May Need' (check ahead of time)				
Removable Scotch Tape				Both
Permanent Scotch Tape				Both
Thumb Tacks or Push Pins if walls are fabric			Make sure to have plenty	Both
Materials for any special activities (I.e. 'silly				Both
Posters				
Principles Poster				Both
8 Wastes Poster				Both
Ground Rules Poster				Both
Any other Posters you may want to bring (ex. Big Data Sheet)				Both
Computerized Resources				
Current State PPT				Both
Future State PPT				Both
Metrics Calculator				Both
Equipment - Check availability at site				
Laptop				
Projector			Lean Office if you need it	Both
Extension cord			"	Both
Power Strip			"	Both
Duct Tape to secure Cord against 'trip hazard'			(Doesn't everyone carry Duct Tape with them?) Lean Office.	Both

APPENDIX F

February 17, 2011

Dr. Walter Lowell
Maine Department of Health And Human Services
221 State Street
State House Station 11
Augusta, ME 04330

Re: Bend the Curve

Dear Dr. Lowell:

Thank you for participating in the second round of the 2010 Innovations in American Government competition. It is gratifying to know that our nation's public sector continues to be so innovative and effective. Accordingly, review teams struggled to select our Top 25 programs. Although your program was not chosen to advance further in this year's Innovations Award competition, I am pleased to report that our evaluators have selected your program to receive designation as a Bright Idea.

The Bright Ideas initiative serves to complement the Innovations in American Government Awards Program by shining a light on noteworthy and promising government programs and practices so that government leaders, public servants, and other individuals can learn about these ideas and adopt initiatives that work. As a Bright Idea, your program will be highlighted on the Ash Center's Government Innovator's Network, and you will receive a seal designating your program as a Bright Idea. All Bright Ideas will also become a part of the Government Innovator's Network open collection of innovations.

The Ash Center is planning a press announcement about this Bright Ideas group for mid-March 2011. At that time, you will be provided with the Bright Ideas seal and information about your program will be posted on the Government Innovators Network. **Please refrain from making any public announcement regarding your program's status until our formal press announcement in March 2011.**

We will be in touch in shortly with further updates about the Bright Ideas process. Should you have questions about the Bright Ideas initiative, or if for some reason you have decided to decline recognition as a Bright Idea, please contact us via email at: BrightIdeas@hks.harvard.edu.

We greatly appreciate your committing the time and thought necessary to present a formidable application. On behalf of the reviewers, members of the Innovations staff, the Ford Foundation, and Harvard University, we wish you continued success in all of your endeavors.

Sincerely,

Christina Marchand
Associate Director for Outreach
Innovations in American Government Program

Kara O'Sullivan
Associate Director for Evaluation
Innovations in American Government Program

79 John F. Kennedy Street
Cambridge, Massachusetts 02138

Founding Donor: The Ford Foundation

www.ash.harvard.edu

REFERENCES

Anderson, Dean, and Linda A. Anderson. *Beyond Change Management: Advanced Strategies for Today's Transformational Leaders*. Jossey-Bass/Pfeiffer, 2011.

Anbari, Frank T. *Aligning Six Sigma Strategy with Current Department Initiatives*. George Washington University.

Babar, Michael, Alastair Levy, and Lenny Mendonca. "Global Trends Affecting the Public Sector." *McKinsey Quarterly Review* (2007).

Bhatia, Nina, and John Drew. "Applying Lean Production to the Public Sector." *McKinsey Quarterly Review* (2006).

Bodek, Norman. *Kaikaku: The Power and Magic of Lean: A Study in Knowledge Transfer*. Vancouver: OCS Press, 2004.

Burton, Terence, and Steven M. Boeder. *The Lean Extended Enterprise: Moving Beyond the Four Walls to Value Stream Excellence*. J. Ross Publishing, 2003.

Cole, Martin, former group chief executive of Accenture's government operating group, and Greg Parson, of Accenture Institute of public service value. "Unlocking Public Value." 1996–2007.

Collins, Jim. *Good to Great and the Social Sectors*. 2005.

Cusumano, Michael, and Kentaro Nobeoka. *Thinking Beyond Lean: How Multi-Project Management is Transforming Product Development at Toyota and Other Companies*. New York: The Free Press, 1998.

Danker, Tony, Thomas Dohrmann, Nancy Killefer, and Lenny Mendonca. "How Can American Government Meet Its Productivity Challenges?" *McKinsey Quarterly Review* (2006).

Dennis, Pascal. *Lean Production Simplified*. New York: Productivity Press, 2002.

Flinchbaugh, Jamie, and Andy Carlino. *The Hitchhiker's Guide to Lean*. Society of Manufacturing Engineers, 2006.

Ford, Henry, *Today and Tomorrow*, Boca Raton, CRC Press, 1988.

George, Michael L. *Lean Six Sigma for Service*. New York: McGraw-Hill, 2003.

George, Michael, David Rowlands, Mark Price, and John Maxey. *Lean Six Sigma*

Pocket Tool Book. New York: McGraw-Hill, 2005.

Gittell, Jody Hoffer. *High Performance Healthcare*. New York: McGraw-Hill, 2009.

Grinnell, Frederick. *Everyday Practice of Science*. Oxford University Press, 2009.

Gross, John M. and Kenneth R. McInnis. *Kanban Made Simple*. New York: American Management Association, 2003.

Greif, Michel. *The Visual Factory*. New York: Productivity Press, 1991.

Hino, Satoshi. *Inside the Mind of Toyota*. Translated by Andrew Dillon. New York: Productivity Press, 2006.

Imai, Masaaki. *Gemba Kaizen: A Commonsense, Low-Cost Approach to Management*. New York: McGraw-Hill, 1997.

Juran, Joseph. National Technical University (NTU) "Quest for Quality" and NTU Special Series "Quality Improvement as a Business Strategy." @1989 William E. Eureka. Tuesday, October 24, 1989. Pages 5 of 137 and 54 of 137 of the October 1989 slide presentations.

Kennedy, Michael. *Product Development for the Lean Enterprise*. Richmond: Oakleaf Press, 2003.

Keyte, Beau, and Drew Locher. *The Complete Lean Enterprise: Value Stream Mapping for Administrative and Office Processes*. New York: Productivity Press, 2004.

King, Bob. *Better Designs in Half the Time*. Goal/QPC, 1989.

Leach, Lawrence P. *Lean Project Management: Eight Principles for Success*. Idaho: Advanced Projects, 2006.

Levinson, William A. *Henry Ford's Lean Vision: Enduring Principles from the First Ford Motor Plant*. New York: Productivity Press, 2002.

Liker, Jeffrey. *The Toyota Way*. McGraw-Hill, 2005.

Liker, Jeffrey, and David Meier. *The Toyota Way Fieldbook*. McGraw-Hill, 2006.

Liker, Jeffrey. *Developing Lean leaders at All Levels*. Lean Leadership Institute, 2014.

Miller, Ken. *We Don't Make Widgets*. Governing Management Series, 2006.

Neave, Henry R. *The Deming Dimension*. Knoxville, TN: SPC Press, 1990.

Reddy-Phillips. Consultants to Organizations. 1988

Robinson, Alan, and Dean Schroeder. *Ideas are Free*. San Francisco: Berrett-Koehler, 2004.

Schein, Edgar, et al., *DEC is Dead, Long Live DEC*. Berrett-Koehler, 2003.

Seddon, John. *Freedom from Command and Control: Rethinking Management for Lean Service*. New York: Productivity Press, 2005.

Seddon, John. *I Want You to Cheat: The Unreasonable Guide to Service and Quality Organizations*. Vanguard Press, 1992.

Seddon, John. *In Pursuit of Quality: The Case Against ISO 9000*. London: Oak Tree Press, 1997.

Tannenbaum, PhD, Senior Faculty. NTL Institute, 1999.

Watanabe, Ken. *Problem Solving 101*. Penguin Group, 2009.

Weisbord, Marvin, and Sandra Janoff. *Future Search: An Action Guide to Finding Common Ground in Organizations and Communications*. San Francisco: Berrett-Koehler, 2000.

Womack, James, and Daniel Jones. *Lean Thinking*. New York: Free Press, 2003.

CPSIA information can be obtained
at www.ICGtesting.com
Printed in the USA
LVHW070316280121
677515LV00004B/37